THE
IRONIC
CHRISTIAN'S
COMPANION

THE
IRONIC
CHRISTIAN'S
COMPANION

Finding the Marks of God's Grace in the World

PATRICK HENRY

Riverhead Books · a member of Penguin Putnam Inc. New York 1999

RIVERHEAD BOOKS
a member of
Penguin Putnam Inc.
375 Hudson Street
New York, NY 10014

Library of Congress Cataloging-in-Publication Data

Henry, Patrick, date.
The ironic Christian's companion: finding the marks
of God's grace in the world / Patrick Henry.
p.   cm.
Includes bibliographical references.
ISBN 1-57322-107-4 (alk. paper)
1. Grace (Theology)   I. Title.
BT761.2.H46   1999   98-33287 CIP

Printed in the United States of America
1   3   5   7   9   10   8   6   4   2

This book is printed on acid-free paper. ∞

BOOK DESIGN BY CHRIS WELCH
TITLE PAGE PHOTO BY MARC YANKUS

for my wife

PAT WELTER

So this can be,
two lifetimes
have conspired
to find resonance,
the dance of a double star.

Contents

THE
IRONIC
CHRISTIAN'S
COMPANION

ON WHAT YOU WILL
(AND WON'T)
FIND IN THIS BOOK

Am I one of them? You say it's for 'ironic Christians.' How do I know if there's any point in my reading further?"

A fair question. And if you require a neat, brief answer, this book is not for you. One of the chief characteristics of an ironic Christian is an instinctive, abiding suspicion of no-loose-ends answers.

Catholic, Pentecostal, Methodist, Orthodox—these kinds of Christians are familiar. But Ironic? I'm not starting a new denomination. I can't remember the moment when I first knew that the term was right, but it serves to identify a way of being Christian that seems strange in these days when the Christians who are the loudest are very sure about many things that might be thought still open for discussion.

An ironic Christian inhabits a world that is more "as if" than "just like," a world fashioned by a God of surprises. The grace of this God is mysterious, sneaky. Some Christians chalk things up much too easily, too quickly, to the grace of God. "There but for the grace of God go I" has the merit of not claiming too much credit for myself, but it implies that I have more of God's grace than the other person.

I trust God's grace but hesitate to identify it in particular cases. It often blindsides me, regularly catches me off guard, seldom hits me square in the face. When I *know* the grace of God, it's nearly always after the fact, usually long afterward.

Grace, as I have experienced it, makes me an ironic Christian. I cannot define "ironic Christian" in a few sentences. If I could, I'd not have bothered writing a book. The only way I can explain "ironic Christian" is to invite you to come with me into a world where I have found, and been found by, the grace of God.

This book is not an owner's manual. I'm not telling you how to fix anything. If you picked the volume off a self-help shelf, somebody put it in the wrong place. The book is a *Companion*—the fancy traditional Latin term is *vademecum,* or "go with me"—a combination of shared wisdom, spiritual resource, antidote to boredom, helper out of jams, teaser of the imagination, and, ideally, a good read.

In some ways, too, this Companion is like a field guide. I'm thinking of Roger Tory Peterson's *Field Guides* to the birds, which, he says, are "designed so that live birds could be readily identified at a distance by their 'field marks.'" I find the term "field marks" especially helpful. I am concerned with what I have come to think of as the field marks of the grace of God. Since I usually discern God's grace at a distance and after the fact, not up close and at the moment, I am always on the lookout for field marks that can be seen in retrospect and from afar. I want to be very clear: In this book, I am not defining the grace of God. I'm saying what I have found it to be like. I make no claim that this Companion is in some universal or objective sense true. I hope it is trustworthy.

Some of what I say is autobiographical in the conventional sense: what I did, how I felt doing it, the reactions of others. I want in these pages to be a companion for you as many writers have been for me. The borders between reading and writing and living are fluid. I do not take time out from life to write, nor do I take time out from life to read. When I quote somebody, I'm not hiding. I'm introducing you to one of my conversation partners.

The grace of God is not linear, hence the absence of chapter numbers. The sections of this book are called "*On* this" rather than "This" because they open up more than they finish off what they're about. I take both cues and comfort from the title of a college admissions brochure that slyly offers *A Question for Every Answer,* and from movie director Jean-Luc Godard's response when another filmmaker, not a fan of modern cinema's haphazard adherence to chronology, harrumphed, "Movies should have a beginning, a middle, and an end": "Certainly, but not necessarily in that order."

The ordering of things in these pages isn't arbitrary, but it isn't sacrosanct either. It makes sense to read straight through. It also makes sense to jump around.

Stay with me, read on. You don't have to know at the start whether you're an ironic Christian. When you're done, you still might not know. Demand for guarantees far exceeds supply. But even if you're a non-ironic Christian, or not Christian at all, you might enjoy the journey. The root meaning of *companion* is "one who eats bread with," not "one who agrees with," and the best traveling parties, beginning with Chaucer's motley band on the way to Canterbury, are those with an uncommon mix of guests.

ON LITTLE
BROWN JOBS

If I say right at the beginning that grace, amazing grace, has brought me safe thus far and will lead me home, it may seem that I am stuffing the rabbit into the hat so I can pull it out later. This book is about the grace of God, but not about magic, and certainly not about anything easy. It's about something simple, that God can be trusted but not taken for granted—a difficult simplicity that I didn't learn in kindergarten or even in college or graduate school. I discovered it along a way that twists and turns, where Yogi Berra's advice, "When you come to a fork in the road, take it," makes perfect sense.

What is it like to find, and be found by, the grace of God in this world? I doubt it's exactly the same for any two people. For me, it's not even the same from day to day. Two divorces and a father's suicide, hardly sufficient trauma to qualify me for Job's league, have been enough trouble to rouse instant suspicion of anyone hawking cheap grace. When churches leave "he descended into hell" out of the Apostles' Creed—to protect Christ's honor, I suppose, or maybe to avoid making the congregation feel bad—I feel cheated. It's where Christ comes to a fork in the road and takes it. Christ's descent into hell is the guarantee of grace.

Over and over again, grace has come as irony: an off-balance deflating of my pride, sometimes as funny as vaudeville slapstick; a gentle dismantling of my despair (when I'm really hopeless nothing is scarier than hope, so grace has to be indirect, sneaky); clarity when I'm too confused and confusion when I'm too clear.

"As if" and "just like"

"It is extraordinary what a difference there is between understanding a thing and knowing it by experience." In this compact sentence, Saint Teresa of Ávila identifies grace as irony: it is the *extraordinary difference.* While the difference isn't usually as sharp as I "was blind but now I see," there is surprise around nearly every corner. If I say that I "understand" something, chances are that I have slipped it into an already stuffed file folder in a drawer that I have opened many times. "Now I understand" too easily equals "Oh, that's familiar after all." Knowing by experience, on the contrary, is very often startling, requiring a new filing cabinet, maybe even a whole new filing system. If astonishment has its effect, understanding itself is dislodged from the familiar. The world I have come to know through my experience is a place fashioned by, loved by, redeemed by a God who won't let us lock the box of surprises.

To be both ironic and Christian is to know, with a knowing deeper than doctrine, the simple, unnerving truth that the visage of faith is not the happy face but the masks of comedy and tragedy, alternating, unpredictably, between laughter and tears, sometimes crying and laughing at the same time, or even, on occasion, crying because it's so funny and laughing because it hurts so much.

An ironic Christian, suspicious of how things seem at first glance, looks at Andres Serrano's notorious "Piss Christ" photograph of a crucifix in a jar of urine and wonders whether the effect is to sully Christ or make piss holy. Being plunged into urine would hardly faze one who has already descended into hell. And if God really became a human being, isn't piss part of the package deal? Some fastidious, non-ironic souls in the early church admitted that Jesus ate (the Gospels told them so), but insisted that he didn't digest, since he would then have had to shit. They couldn't bear to think that God's swaddling clothes might be dirty and need changing.

In Serrano's photograph, what looks like crystal-clear blasphemy makes, on deeper reflection, a profoundly faithful point. It works the other way too. The Golden Rule, "Do unto others as you would have them do unto you," widely regarded as the best thing Jesus ever said, could surely, we suppose, be classified as undeniably good. But the Golden Rule can wreak havoc on relationships. I was once called upon professionally to handle a tense standoff between two people, he an off-the-charts extravert, she an off-the-charts introvert. He interpreted her withdrawn behavior to mean what it would mean if he acted in the same way: "Please come to my assistance." He (the extravert) did unto her (the introvert) what he would have done unto him—and things got progressively worse. He thought he was being a help, she thought he was being a pest. In a world of Myers-Briggs personality types, the Golden Rule must be applied with caution.

Many Christians are sure that God made a "just like" world, where blasphemy is blasphemy—"I know it when I see it"—and faithfulness is measured by the fervor with which one asserts the bumper-sticker litany: "The Bible: God said it, I believe it, that settles it." They recoil from an "as if" world. They can imagine nothing to be said in favor of the Serrano photograph or against the Golden Rule. The ironic Christian, who knows an "as if" world and the God who made it, certainly does not claim that all blasphemy is masked piety or that all Scripture must be taken with a grain of salt but does insist that very few answers are given in advance, and even those that are may not be easy to understand.

Once upon a time the term "Christian" meant wider horizons, a larger heart, minds set free, room to move around. But these days "Christian" sounds pinched, squeezed, narrow. Many people who identify themselves as Christians seem to have leapfrogged over life, short-circuited the adventure. When "Christian" appears in a headline, the story will probably be about lines drawn, not about boundaries expanded.

This book is for Christians who think that what was true

once upon a time can be true again and should be true always: curiosity, imagination, exploration, adventure are not preliminary to Christian identity, a kind of booster rocket to be jettisoned when spiritual orbit is achieved. They are part of the payload.

We are all explorers, telling each other what new things we have seen and heard. I will report to you some of what I have come to know. I take my cue from Anne Sexton: "A story, a story! / (Let it go, let it come.)" Notice that she does not add "and I will explain it to you." A writer friend of mine says that the best advice she ever got was "Show, don't tell." Though I do not have the poet's trust to let the story just go and come— I can't always resist the urge to tell—I suspect that I am closest to the truth when I am least intrusive. One of Anne Sexton's unexplained stories *shows* that she knew something about God that I have come to know too. She imagines playing poker with God, sure that she will win because she holds a royal straight flush, stunned when God holds five aces: "A wild card had been announced/but I had not heard it."

Maybe you won't see the same things that I do, or you'll see the same things in another way. My effort to recover and restate a Christian vision is only one of many. Such efforts are taking place in pulpits, library carrels, publishing houses, in soup kitchens and homeless shelters and AIDS hospices, in refugee camps and Sunday school classes and church choir rehearsal rooms, in monasteries, prayer breakfasts, potluck suppers—wherever people are trying to figure out and figure forth the Christian life in a world not particularly interested in a Christian agenda shaped by the ironic, wild-card God.

Annie Dillard, appalled at the blandness and smug self-assurance that characterize some Christian worship, says that when we go into church "we should all be wearing crash helmets. Ushers should issue life preservers and signal flares; they should lash us to our pews." I write mainly for Christians who know what Dillard is getting at, and who will be glad to hear that there are honest ways to be Christian besides being surer than they can be. I don't understand Christians who have everything figured out, and I don't envy them. I get nervous when things stay put, are cut and dried. Having it all figured out in the name of Christ is no more appealing to me than is the "explained world" that a Soviet writer thanked Lenin for bequeathing him. I would like it to be said of me, as has been written about one of my heroes, Czech Republic playwright and president Václav Havel: "Everything interests and astonishes him as if he had just seen it for the first time." "*As if*—for the first time": an ironic Christian knows new, knows fresh, knows surprise, but does not know it all. This book is about a Christian way of knowing. It is not about *the* Christian way, but I suspect that I am not the only one for whom the Christian way talked about here rings true.

Knowing and interpreting

Since age two I've been waltzing up and down with the question of life's meaning. And I am obliged to report that the answer changes from week to week. When I know the answer, I know it absolutely; as soon as I know that I know it, I know that I know nothing. About seventy percent of the time my conclusion is that there is a grand design." Maya Angelou's seventy percent is, for me, about the best we can hope for. If I thought I had to be sure all the time, I would despair, and if I were sure all the time, I would be a menace to myself and everyone around me. What Richard Preston, in his electrifying account of an outbreak of the Ebola virus, *The Hot Zone,* says of biology, I find to be generally true of the world, God's world: "In biology, nothing is clear, everything is too complicated, everything is a mess, and just when you think you understand something, you peel off a layer and find deeper complications beneath. Nature is anything but simple." Simplicities lurk in the complications, but they are difficult simplicities, and you can't—at least I can't—get to them by an end run around the complications.

"A Christian way of knowing" is not the same as "a Christian interpretation of experience." I hesitate to claim that I can offer "a Christian interpretation" of anyone's experience, including my own. I do not step back, survey my life, and say, "Here is evidence of the grace of God." Once, I proposed "a Christian interpretation" of someone else's experience—I quoted Romans 8:28—"We know that in everything God works for good"—to a girlfriend who had just told me of her young brother's death from leukemia several years before—and my relationship with her abruptly ended. "A Christian way of knowing" is characterized by candor and concreteness, not theological correctness or pious sentiment. It acknowledges, even revels in, what C. S. Lewis calls "the roughness and density of life."

We are mysteries to each other, to ourselves. We can, and constantly do, talk about our experiences, and as soon as we start talking, we are interpreting. But it is one thing to interpret experience by talking about it and another to take the story told and give it "a Christian interpretation." I am as wary of Christian spin doctors as I am of their political counterparts. I find myself always in a position like that of the Soviet Union as described by an official in mid-1990: "We are trying to sail a ship and simultaneously rebuild it. We don't have a spare ship to step into for a moment and sail." A Christian interpretation, as something different from the story I tell, is a spare ship I don't have.

We make our way into and through the world we see depending on perspective and frames of reference. Seeing is believing, we are taught, but it is equally true that believing is seeing. The world that I see, the world that I know, did not come to me in an instant. It is not fixed yet, but it has recognizable and fairly consistent features. Its contours are shaped both by what happens "out there" and by what happens inside me.

Habit and change

I have come through many years of psychotherapy convinced that I am not so much a rational animal as a creature of habit. When change comes it is seldom in response to good ideas or persuasive arguments. I change when my imagination catches sight of a new possibility. Such sights usually sneak up on me. Sometimes they catapult me into conversion. The new possibilities are almost always, after the fact, "obvious," and I can't believe that it was so hard to get to where I could recognize them. But *get to where* is not just a figure of speech. It names a journey that can seem, on the way, a descent into hell. I know what Saint Augustine is talking about: "Lord, you turned my attention back to myself. You took me up from behind my own back where I had placed myself because I did not wish to observe myself, and you set me before my face." "From behind my own back *where I had placed myself*": it's not as simple as gazing in the mirror. It's more like being pushed through the Looking Glass.

Often I would go to a therapy session full of "reporting" that I thought would excite the therapist. Many things had happened during the week that I knew were "significant," and, even more satisfying, "from behind my own back where I had placed myself" I "knew" what they "meant." I was sure the therapist would be proud of me for the evident progress I was making (and making people proud of me I had developed to a high art). Invariably, when I rattled on in this fashion she showed no trace of heightened interest, and I would leave feeling the hour had been wasted.

Other times I would go to a session convinced that nothing at all had happened in the intervening week. I was stuck. I was sure I would bore the therapist. Invariably, these were the most electric sessions. The desperate urge to self-preservation stymied growth. It was when I gave up the effort to interpret my experience, the effort to control the therapy process itself, that I began to know, with the therapist's skillful help, what had happened and was happening, and—the intrusion of grace—what *could* happen.

In countless other encounters as well, I have come to know how many ways there are to say the same thing, and how many different things an apparently "same" way of speaking can mean. People use words I would choke on and mean things that I endorse, or use my terminology in ways that I would expect to make them gag. Christian truth as conventionally expressed has for many people, including me from time to time, gone flat. Kathleen Norris, in *Amazing Grace: A Vocabulary of Faith,* has rejuvenated some of what she calls the "scary words," theological terms like "eschatology" and "Christ" and "repentance" and even "God." She says these words initially repelled her when she returned to church after being away for twenty years. She felt them excluding her, not inviting her in. For me, too, who never left the church, the terminology needs the kind of jump start that Norris provides. And she offers a grammar of faith as well as a vocabulary. She restores the words to their natural habitat—storytelling—where they dart like trout in a stream and soar like herons on the wind. By insisting that every Christian is a theologian, with a word about God (that's what the term theology means), she helps free us from the kind of self-imposed plight I saw in a devoted church member who said in my hearing, "I never realized that the position on free will and predestination the minister outlined in this morning's sermon is what I'm supposed to believe. Now I'll have to start believing it."

This book is written from Christian faith, but little in its form will seem familiar from books on theology or even on spirituality, although I have lived the tradition as long as I can remember and have studied and taught it for decades. Christian doctrine is in my bloodstream. My father and both grandfathers were pastors, and my great-grandfather was a lay preacher. The Christian story is woven into the fabric of my memories, my hopes, my fears, my desires, my dreads, my fantasies, my dreams. The way I think and feel, the way I read, the way I write are steeped in the Bible, in the words and tunes of hymns, and are crisscrossed with Christian terminology. But I no longer take the faith for granted, though I grew up so close to the life of the church that I was literally incredulous when one of my friends in high school said, "You know that there is no God." By incredulous, I don't mean simply that I didn't agree with him. I believed that his opinion was impossible to have. At that time I could not imagine that there might be atheists. For some people, spiritual maturity means coming to know God. For me and, I suspect, others like me, so steeped in the church that "knowing God" came easy—too easy—spiritual maturing has meant acknowledging that it is possible to honestly not know God, and even to dishonestly know God.

There are vast regions between the wasteland of Macbeth's despair—"Life is a tale told by an idiot, full of sound and fury, signifying nothing"—and the dream land of "Christian" optimism, in which our problems will all be solved if we will just turn everything over to Jesus. I have gazed into both those lands and have been tempted to pass over into them. The temptations are similar—despair can be as alluring as optimism, for both promise a kind of clarity—but grace has held me back in this world where, for better or worse, most of us live most of the time. Abraham, who left home to go he knew not where; Moses, who knew where he was going but did not get there; and Paul, who saw through a glass darkly and kept pressing on toward the goal, give me courage.

Little brown jobs

Some years ago I learned from Diane Ackerman, in an article mainly about the most distinctive of all birds, the penguin, that even "avid bird-spotters know how easy it is to get confused about birds," and that they have a catch-all category for ones they do not recognize: "most birds are what birders call 'L.B.J.s.'" You might think, on hearing "that is an L.B.J.," that you are being asked to imagine some similarity between the bird-in-question and the thirty-sixth president of the United States. But you are not. You are being told that what you see is a "little brown job," a bird whose identity the expert does not know. I find the world full of L.B.J.s, and I distrust guides, whether religious or political or psychological or any other kind, who claim to know what everything is, who don't acknowledge "how easy it is to get confused about" whatever it is they are looking at.

I want my contribution to Christian theology to be the

Doctrine of Little Brown Jobs, a doctrine that encompasses many things. There are events that some Christians would tell me are clearly the will of God, but that look to me like little brown jobs. At least once a week on the nightly news someone who has just survived a car wreck or earthquake or some other calamity looks upward and says, "Somebody was sure looking out for me!" But what about those who were not so looked out for? Conversely, there are events that cynics would tell me are clear signs of life's absurdity, but that look to me like little brown jobs. My father's suicide doesn't make sense to me, but I don't know enough about it to draw a conclusion about the meaning, or lack of meaning, of life. Calling a spade a spade is a trait we are taught to admire in people. I value especially those who put candor and concreteness together and call a little brown job a little brown job, and don't consider it their, or my, Christian duty to claim to know more than we do.

I could launch immediately into an analysis of scriptural passages that anchor the Doctrine of Little Brown Jobs, and in the course of this book I will offer some instances. I start not with the Bible, however, but with an odd and revealing sounding of our culture taken by *Life* magazine in 1988. Forty-nine contemporary "wise men and women" were asked to write a few lines of reflection on the question "Why are we here?" We are not told how the authors of the article, "The Meaning of Life," were picked, and one might wonder why the Reagans' White House astrologer and Oliver North made the list. It is something of a reassuring surprise to find eight identifiable religious figures (Elie Wiesel, Raimon Panikkar, Robert

McAfee Brown, the Dalai Lama, Norman Vincent Peale, Harold Kushner, Seyyed Hossein Nasr, and Tu Wei-Ming) and only four sports luminaries (Muhammad Ali, Mike Ditka, Janet Evans, and Kareem Abdul-Jabbar), but among the eight, where there had apparently been some care to achieve balance (two Jews, one Catholic, two Protestants, one Buddhist, one Muslim, one Confucian), there is no woman and no black, and the Roman Catholic, Panikkar, is identified simply as a "Hindu scholar."

In earlier eras almost everyone, if asked "Why are we here?" would have made mention of God. But only twelve of the forty-nine "wise men and women" use the name of God in a way more or less familiar to people who go to church. Two of the dozen are Jews, three are Muslims; Norman Vincent Peale is not among them, and Oliver North and Mike Ditka are. Christ is named once, by the (Roman Catholic) Hindu scholar, and there is a quotation from the words of Jesus in the remarks of singer Willie Nelson, but the words are identified as from Matthew with no reference to the one who spoke them. Prayer, whether by name or concept or practice, puts in no appearance at all.

The term "church" is used in the compound "churchgoer" by Robert McAfee Brown in a poignant reference to a recently deceased friend. "Church" by itself is mentioned only once, and not favorably: "We are here to unlearn the teachings of the church, state and our educational system," says writer Charles Bukowski—who then, it should be added, goes on to declare, in a more positive vein, "We are here to drink beer." Psychologist Julian Jaynes dismisses religion as primitive when

he relegates "hallucinated voices called gods" to the experience of "early human beings." Comedian Jackie Mason dismisses it as psychotic: "People call it truth, religion; I call it
insanity, the denial of death as the basic truth of life." Mason's
comment is a sign that traditional religion has simply dropped
off the screen; his target is not Christian or Jewish theology
but Shirley MacLaine.

It is refreshing to come upon a sharp, acerbic remark like
that of Jose Martinez: "We're here to die, just live and die. I
drive a cab. I do some fishing, take my girl out, pay taxes, do a
little reading, then get ready to drop dead. You've got to be
strong about it. Life is a big fake. Nobody gives a damn." This
statement resonates better with the clear-eyed plain speech of
the Bible than does the more conventionally religious language of social psychologist Kenneth Ring: "The meaning of
life has something to do with realizing that our essence is perfect love, then going on to live our lives upon that truth, experiencing each day as a miracle and every act as sacred." I
suspect that Jose Martinez, with his energetic, if negatively expressed, spirituality is closer to "experiencing each day as a
miracle and every act as sacred" than are we who claim, often
rather blandly, that "our essence is perfect love" and that we
"live our lives upon that truth."

I'm not as gloomy as the cab driver (though on occasion I
have been), but I would probably find his company more con-
genial than that of the apostles of positive thinking. He has a
refreshing willingness to call a little brown job a little brown
job. There is a spiritual parallel between him and my friend Father Godfrey Diekmann, OSB, of Saint John's Abbey in Min-

nesota, who sank up to his hips in a swamp while gathering watercress and had to be pulled out by a truck hoist. In his Christmas letter that year he said that after more than fifty years of monastic life, "What bothers me is that during the entire ordeal of about twenty-five minutes I didn't have a single pious thought!" The tone of his sentence suggests that it didn't bother him a bit.

Few of the *Life* commentators take their bearings from the Bible and Christ. While I would be happy if more of them did, I do not favor a quick reassertion of confident Christian claims. The imminence of the third millennium is encouraging Christians to wax eloquent—too eloquent, by my reckoning—about the prospects for church and world. We are still in the midst of a long stretch of what the liturgy calls "ordinary time," or a time like the days after Christmas, when, in the words of W. H. Auden, "the Spirit must practise his scales of rejoicing" in a subdued fashion. By making a big deal of the millennium, by strapping grace to the calendar, we are setting ourselves up for disappointment. We would be wiser to classify the millennium as a little brown job.

Liberty, death, and the crazy machine

You may have picked this book up because of my name. (If I saw a new book by Alexander Hamilton or George Washington on the shelf, I'd be curious.) I may come by the name honestly, though probably not as honestly as I used to think. My grandfather, also named Patrick, as were his grandfather and his son, my father, was adamant that the line went

straight back to the revolutionary orator. However, a recent remark of my aunt sent me to materials in a file that show some
uncertainty as to whether the line is direct. Records of Henrys
who moved from Virginia to Tennessee and then to Texas in
the early nineteenth century are hard to find and to verify. The
probability of some connection is enhanced by the fact that
the Patriot had seventeen children; he must have descendants
all over the place. But who I used to think was my great-great-
great-great-great-grandfather may have been my that-many-
greats-uncle, and the relation could be even more remote than
that.

Rather to my surprise, this possible shift from one branch of
the Henry family tree to another has had no detectable effect
on my sense of who I am. It has deprived me of an easy conversation opener, but that opening itself seldom led to any
response other than, "Oh, that's interesting," or the disconcerting, "Liberty or death: that gives you something to live by,
doesn't it?" But I still take more than casual interest in the Patriot and his influence. And what truly astonishes me is the
discovery that my preference for a "both/and"—or at least a
"maybe"—response to the complexity of the world can be
traced right back to those revolutionary times.

Patrick Henry's ringing declaration, "Give me liberty or
give me death," arguably the best-known phrase in American
history, is the ultimate either/or, and helps account for the
reverence in which he is held by right-wing militia groups.
But Patrick Henry lived for more than two decades after the
Revolution. For much of that time he was governor of Virginia and directed the force of his rhetoric against the pro-

posed federal Constitution. He judged that without the protection of a Bill of Rights, citizens under such a government would be in danger of a tyranny to match the one that his earlier speeches had helped defeat.

I cannot decide which I value more highly: Patrick Henry's role in the Revolution itself or his role in assuring that the Constitution has its first ten amendments. I can decide that I prefer one of his later statements, from the year 1791, to the "Give me liberty or give me death" of 1775. It is in a letter to the young and newly elected Senator James Monroe. Henry has been asked to cooperate with some of those whom he formerly fought on the issue of the Constitution, and he says: "The Form of Government into which my Countrymen determined to place themselves, had my Enmity, yet as we are one & all embarked, it is natural to care for the crazy Machine, at least so long as we are out of Sight of a Port to refit." For that Patrick Henry, the 1775 world of birds with clear and distinct field marks gave way, by 1791, to a world of little brown jobs. He makes much the same point with the ship image that was made 199 years later by the Soviet official quoted earlier who, on the eve of the most radical political reorientation of our lifetime, the collapse of the Soviet empire, said, "We don't have a spare ship to step into."

How to fashion a new experiment in human government: this was the momentous issue that faced the earlier Patrick Henry. The task of this Patrick Henry, two centuries later, is more modest: to offer a way of knowing that increases life's abundance. Liberty is my theme, too, but what I can report is that relinquishing control enhances liberty (though without a guarantee of happiness). The crazy machine of the world, this ship that we are simultaneously sailing and trying to rebuild without a spare ship to step into, is a good (though not easy) place to live. Little brown jobs need be neither ugly ducklings nor magnificent swans. They can just be little brown jobs.

ON WHEN IT IS

O nce upon a time—it was March 26, 1975—my finger slipped as I typed a letter. I sat transfixed. In an instant I was transported to the middle of the 198th century: "March 26, 19756." Alice down the hole to Wonderland, the Pevensy children through the wardrobe to Narnia, Captain Janeway and her Starship *Voyager* crew suddenly in a distant quadrant of the galaxy could not have been any more surprised. "Once upon a time"—I use the traditional fairy-tale opener, even though the date is known, because at that precise moment my imagination was sprung free from the trap of time as I had learned to calculate it.

When was long ago?

W e who study human history have been reminded often enough by colleagues in the natural sciences that on

the grand scales of anthropological, or biological, or geological, or galactic, or cosmological time, human history is at best
the blink of an eye. Stephen Jay Gould takes the paleontolo-
gist's long view: "The human species has inhabited this planet
for only 250,000 years or so—roughly .0015 percent of the
history of life, the last inch of the cosmic mile. The world
fared perfectly well without us for all but the last moment of
earthly time."

The slip of my finger on the typewriter revealed, in the
blink of an eye, that history itself as it has unfolded so far is but
a fragment of what it would be from the vantage-point of the
198th century. Before my typographical error—an error that
would have passed unremarked a few years later, in the age of
the word-processor delete button—I thought of the age of the
apostles, the first church councils, the medieval cathedrals as "a
long time ago." Ever after the error, I have known that we are
part of the early church. To the historian of the 198th century,
we of the first twenty centuries will occupy no greater a por-
tion—ten percent—of the church's past than do the Christians
of the first two centuries from our perspective. That extra 6 in
19756 put me in my place. The notion that we are late in the
story no longer makes much sense to me. Tradition is what we
are creating even more than it is what we depend on.

This putting me in my place is what I have come to expect
of God. I did not plan it, organize it. I did not even want it.
Perhaps in some sense I needed it, though I would not have
said so. Nothing is ever the same again; neither, however, is
anything solved. It is a kind of enchantment, but an enchantment that is a waking up, not a dozing or a drifting.

To be sure, when we are put in our place we are given a valuable gift—freedom from a constricting reliance on the authority of decisions made in the past (for example, for nearly two thousand years all Catholic and Orthodox clergy have been male; but that is *only* the first two thousand years). However, with the gift comes a corresponding responsibility—we are as answerable to God as the apostles were for what we make of the tradition, what we pass on to the generations after ours. I could interpret the slip of my finger to mean that what we call "the early church" does not deserve so much respect after all. But this is what it means to me: We in our own time deserve the same respect we have been giving to what we call "the early church"—our authority *and responsibility* are not less than theirs, for we are, with them, members of the early church. And since the finger can *always* slip on the keyboard, those historians in the year 19756, and their successors in 197563, will also be part of the early church.

If yesterday's no is today's yes, maybe today's no will be tomorrow's yes

To find myself in the early church, where we are fashioning doctrine, not just receiving it and handing it on, affects my view of another vexed question besides that of women's ordination. During the semester in which I was catapulted into the 198th century, I participated as one of several instructors, from various departments, in a student-run course at Swarthmore College on homosexuality. I was responsible for only one small segment of the study, the historical and contemporary attitudes of religion, and I was struck by the degree to which the students in the course, both the gay ones and the straight ones, believed that what the churches do and say still has major significance for our society and, in some instances, for themselves.

In the summer of 1975, immediately following that semester, I was invited to preach at the Swarthmore Presbyterian Church, of which I was a member. The Presbyterian General Assembly had recently rejected a report of the Presbyterian Gay Caucus on the grounds that "the Scripture as understood in our Reformed tradition does not condone [the] sexual orientation and life-style" of homosexuals. From the pulpit I acted on my conviction that gay people in the church should not have to stand alone as advocates in their own cause.

In the sermon, I presented arguments from the Bible, from ethics, and from the nature of the church itself for accepting homosexual orientation and practice. There were then, and still are, many persons who draw exactly the opposite conclusion from their study of these areas. I drew also on my experience. I said that I had come to know some gay people fairly well, and it was simply unthinkable to me to exclude them from full fellowship in the church. By full fellowship I meant welcome without judgment, without footnotes—indeed, it meant getting beyond the point of even thinking in terms of "welcoming." It was a serious indictment of the church that there had to be a Gay "Caucus" at all. "The church is the church," I said, "where dividing walls of hostility are broken down, where we are all one in the body of Christ, where it is Christ himself who welcomes all of us equally, and we do not decide shall we or shall we not welcome this one or that one." Things seemed to me to be very mixed up when it was in my work as a professor in the academy, and not in my active membership in the church, that I came to appreciate the identity, the dignity, and the proper pride of gay people. After all, Jesus spoke (John 14:2) of many rooms in God's house, not of many closets.

As worshipers left the sanctuary following the service, some glowered, some said that it was about time somebody spoke up in the way I had. A few called me brave, though as a tenured college professor preaching a single guest sermon I had nothing to lose.

The slip of my finger on the typewriter four months earlier and the sermon I had just preached were connected, though I didn't realize it at the time. What put those two moments together was my father's suicide in May 1983. The putting together didn't happen immediately. Only recently have I come to see that by imagining myself in an earlier time, I know by analogy the rejection that gay Christians experience.

For hundreds of years Christians whose relatives killed themselves were told by the church that those relatives had committed an "intrinsically evil" act, an unforgivable sin, and that they were in the place where Dante's *Divine Comedy* puts them, the seventh circle of hell. As recently as 1912, *The Catholic Encyclopedia* declared that the church "condemns the act as a most atrocious crime and, in hatred of the sin and to arouse the horror of its children, denies the suicide Christian burial." Few churches these days say anything so heartless (the 1983 Roman Catholic *Code of Canon Law* quietly drops suicides from the list of those denied church funeral rites), and I have not been burdened with a theology that writes my father off as lost. But I could imagine what it was like in earlier times for people like me: tormented by the image—drawn by those who were acknowledged to *know*—of an unbridgeable chasm between God and the one they loved.

As my imagination took hold, I became angry. What does it mean about Christian certainties that they so often change? By what right, during all those generations, did the church, which now acknowledges that there is hope for suicides and no longer segregates their corpses, presume to know otherwise? It is not enough to say that doctrine develops, or that it takes time for the church to come to full understanding, or that historical perspective precludes holding earlier generations to our standards. History teaches us to be skeptical of our certainties, especially when those certainties exclude people unlike us.

I believe that a hundred years from now the declaration that homosexuality is "intrinsically disordered," and even odious in the sight of God, will be regarded by most Christians as a curiosity of a bygone age. I believe that our time's burdening of gay people with declarations that what they experience *as their identity* offends God will be regretted, as we regret an earlier time's declaration that suicides are in hell. The recognition that being gay is not a "choice," that it is not "unnatural," that gay people are not "adopting a life-style" but are simply living their lives, a recognition supported by much scientific evidence, will, I believe, eventually be as persuasive as was the recognition that Copernicus and Galileo were, after all, right.

It is not a hundred years from now, and I may be wrong about the way things will develop, but I ask those who are absolutely certain of God's disapproval of homosexuality to imagine a future in which their descendants wonder how they could have been so sure.

When is it now?

Fifteen years after a typographical error catapulted me eighteen millennia forward and radically changed the way I answer the question, When was long ago? a trip I took made me wonder whether I even know when it is right now.

The travel agent's voice was tinged with misgiving as she repeated my proposed itinerary: "Bangkok, Tel Aviv, Geneva? First time I've ever tried to put those on one ticket!" Her determination trumped her skepticism, and she found a way for me to accept invitations from friends in Thailand, Israel, and Switzerland. In February 1990, I started around the world.

The memories of place are vivid and clearly etched, while the contrasts of place stretch credulity: Can all this variety really be part of the same world? But during my three weeks of travel, the question, Where am I? was less insistent than "When is it?"

There were all those hours on airplanes, the long hauls virtually indistinguishable from one another since I happened to catch each flight when the movie showing was *Indiana Jones and the Last Crusade.* I circled the globe with Harrison Ford and Sean Connery plotting pursuit of the Holy Grail. Then there were the relativities of tomorrow, today, and yesterday.

Thailand is thirteen hours later than Minnesota, and for my eight days there I could have called back any time before one p.m. and said, "Don't be anxious about tomorrow; I've seen it, and it's all right."

But flights long enough to have dinner, snack, and breakfast between stops, and a whirligig of time zones, were only the surface of time's mystery. The substance is the centuries.

The Thai alphabet bears no relation to ours, so the words on billboards were opaque to me, but I kept seeing the figure 33, or sometimes 2533. I learned that it is not a lottery number, not a radio station call number, not a phone number, but *when it is:* the year 2533, a third of the way through the 26th century. Thailand occasionally has to acknowledge that much of the rest of the world measures time from the birth of Jesus, but when Thais think about when it really is, they measure from the birth of the Buddha.

The *Jerusalem Post* had three dates on its masthead: 1990, 5750 (Jewish reckoning from the creation of the world), and 1410 (Muslim reckoning from the year of Muhammad's migration from Mecca to Medina).

Was I in the 26th century, the 20th, the 58th, or the 15th? When our part of the world is soon in some sort of frenzy as "the third millennium" dawns, others, for whom that millennium is already more than half gone, or three millennia ago, or still more than half a millennium in the future, may well wonder what all the fuss is about. My encounter with other calendars has run a highlighter through Jesus' caution: "Of that day or that hour no one knows, not even the angels in heaven, nor the Son, but only the Father" (Mark 13:32). January 1, 2000 (or 2001, which many careful scholars have pointed to as the true beginning of the millennium, since there was no year zero; or maybe it has already been, in 1996 or 1997, since there is the further complication that Jesus' birth was probably in 4 B.C.E.), will be worth a special New Year's party, but the theological thermostat should be set low.

It was providential that one who had been cast into such chronological chaos should make a final stop in Switzerland, time's native habitat. In the center of Geneva Airport stands a digital clock, operated by signals from a satellite, that is accurate to within one second in three hundred centuries. Even if I was oscillating between the 15th and 58th centuries, that clock would be off by no more than thirteen-hundredths of a second. As I stood there I thought, "Finally, within tolerable limits of uncertainty, I know *when it is!*" Several weeks later, after I had returned home, a friend, on hearing this tale, responded to my "when it is" with the query, "And did it matter?"

What is coming?

If a slip of the finger collapsed the distance between the present and long ago, if a trip around the world dislodged the present from the calendar I was used to so that I am no longer sure "when" it is "now," a conversation between two friends, among the brightest Christians I know, alerted me to radically different expectations about what is coming. One began talking, perfectly naturally and without the slightest hint that he might be saying anything odd, about the human prospect over the next million years or so. Granted, he could not speak with a lot of knowledge about what that prospect would be, but he was entirely at ease with the notion that even the 198th century would be part of the earliest beginnings.

The other friend, hearing this, was stunned: "I have always thought that the story is just about over." For him, the human story has already played out most of its options, and God will ring down the final curtain on human history soon—though maybe not within our lifetime. For this friend, it is unlikely that there are even as many acts to come as there have already been. He would have thought that the U.S. Department of Energy was squandering effort and money when it commissioned a study of how to create warnings that will survive and be understood as long as existing nuclear waste dumps remain toxic, until at least the year 12,000. The DOE asked: How can any message be transmitted to human beings of the 120th century? Conveying written information over a 10,000-year span has never been tried; Sumerian tablets date back only half that long. Among the suggestions: ringing a dump with a "modern Stonehenge" into which huge cartoon narratives depicting the danger of the nuclear material are etched. But this problem of long-term communication is worth worrying about only if the human story has at least another hundred centuries to go.

Each of these views—the story has barely begun, the story is just about over—can claim strong roots in Christian tradition. From the difference between these two views many misunderstandings and disagreements flow. Do we expect God to act fast or slow? Does it make sense to work for a better society? If the story is nearly over, probably not, though there is the contrary example of Martin Luther, who is reported—in an apocryphal, though characteristic, story—to have replied, when asked what he would do if he knew the world would end tomorrow, "I would plant an apple tree."

On this question, more than on any other among the perennial puzzles of Christian thought and feeling, I practice F. Scott Fitzgerald's juggling act: "the ability to hold two opposed ideas in the mind at the same time, and still retain the ability to function." Some Christians would tell me that the Bible is crystal clear: The story is nearly over on the soon-to-be late great planet earth, so any difficulty I have accepting that conclusion is not an honest admission of ambiguity but a prideful refusal to accept divine revelation. But the Bible is *not* clear on this point—John's Gospel, for instance, leaves the story open to an indefinitely extended future—even though an impressive arsenal of proof-texts can be, and frequently is, assembled.

My instincts are with the friend who imagines the next million years, but what inhibits my leaping out there with him is not theology. Rather, my imagination reaches its limit well before a million years have gone by. Science fiction is an aerobic workout for my imagination, increasing its endurance and expanding its capacity. But as I watch *Star Trek: The Next Generation* and realize that the society portrayed there, in some ways so familiar but in others so strange, is projected only into the twenty-fourth century, and then calculate that it takes 9,976 more *centuries* beyond that to reach the year one million, my imagination balks. And, of course, a million itself is an arbitrary boundary. Why stop there?

Friends tell me I am making an unreal problem for myself, that whether Christ returns in the year 2000 or the year 2,000,000 is beside the point, the point being that the story is God's and its culmination is the return of Christ.

But that does not end my puzzlement. Our sense of who Christ is and will be and what Christ does and will do is determined in part by our understanding of the story into which he came and into which he will come again. What if, as the story develops further, Klingons and Vulcans and Romulans and Bajorans come upon the scene? What if androids like Commander Data are constructed? What are we to make of the status in the scheme of redemption of a half-Vulcan, half-human such as Mr. Spock, or a human/betazoid cross like Counselor Deanna Troi? And does the almost total absence of references to the Bible, Christ, or the church in the *Star Trek* episodes reflect simply a producer's wariness of sticky religious matters, or is it a plausible indirect prediction of the eclipse of Christianity?

Most intriguing and disturbing of all (because the question does not depend on our finding new civilizations where no one has boldly gone before), what effect on the story would—will—major changes in human nature itself have? Much can change in the next million years, just the way much has changed in the past million years. Neanderthals were still around only 35,000 years ago. Did Christ die for them? And change will probably accelerate as human beings become increasingly clever at investigating and manipulating the basic determinants of characteristics and character. Theologians and ethicists should plead for extreme caution in matters of genetic experimentation (genetic differences between species are remarkably small), but such experimentation is certain to happen, and then what role in the divine scheme will we assign to the beings that come into the world? The role of Christ in interreligious dialogue is difficult enough. What will interspecies dialogue be like?

The question of how much time is left is not for me mainly a philosophical or theological or moral problem, though all these issues play a part in what for me *is* the problem: one of imagination. I feel at one with at least some Christians who expect that the story will be over before the century of the voyages of the starship *Enterprise.* I feel at one with at least some Christians who think that the Apostles and we and Captain Jean-Luc Picard are all simply part of the first paragraph of the prologue. These two groups have ideas of God and Christ that some critics would say are incompatible. I hold both ideas and "still retain the ability to function." How is this?

The crack of now and the crawl of the ages

First, the experience of time is anything but uniform. Clock time and calendar time often bear no relation to how time seems. We can measure time with pinpoint precision (remember the Geneva Airport clock), but in the throes of depression time can compress, squeeze you breathless. "Soon" and "later" are hard to schedule, and while "within a couple of hundred years" and "in a million years or so" hardly seem equivalent expressions—they stretch the usual range of the common expression "sooner or later"—time as experienced lets me say that *very soon* and *much later* may not be all that different. The reality of God sometimes has the crack of now, sometimes the crawl of the ages. Gerard Manley Hopkins caught the distinction in a line about the Damascus Road conversion of Saint Paul and the long, tortuous spiritual journey recounted in Saint Augustine's *Confessions:* "at once, as once at a crash Paul,/Or as Austin, a lingering-out sweet skill." Cracking, crawling—the measurement of time can seem astonishingly inexact.

Second, time can be visualized, too, with similar surprises. My professional work as a historian has overturned my commonsensical notions of what past, present, and future are like. The "Prelude" to Thomas Mann's giant four-part novel, *Joseph and His Brothers,* evokes a paradoxical discovery that I had made many times but had never recognized: The deeper you go into the past, the broader your horizon becomes. I don't mean simply that you are reduced to speculation when you have only hieroglyphs and pottery to work with. I mean that investigating history can bring on vertigo. Mann expected that as he moved further and further back in time, beyond the reach of available sources, his view would finally narrow to the vanishing point. What he found instead was the abyss of the past, its limitless vastness. I suspect that if Mann had lived long enough to read Stephen Hawking's paradoxical description of the universe, in *A Brief History of Time,* as "finite without boundary," he would have delightedly said, "The universe is just like history."

The present is also various and vast. When people say that they want to talk about current events because such things are more understandable, easier to grasp, than history, they are not speaking for me. Are these the best of times or the worst of times or just run-of-the-mill times? I find this question no easier to answer than why the Roman Empire fell, or why it rose in the first place.

So, the past is an abyss and the present a puzzle. Surely, then, the future is open, harder to pin down than even the past. This is what I thought until, in 1991, I was asked to write an article speculating about the future of the ecumenical movement, this century's reversal of the millennium-long tendency of churches to come apart and condemn one another. I started jotting down features of the current scene from which I might extrapolate, and I expected that my thoughts would go off in a million directions. What happened though, was a rapid narrowing of focus to three projections, about increasing inclusiveness, suppler language and a greater variety of images, and the revitalizing of tradition by reactivated imaginations. These projections are quite general, of course, but I was astonished to discover that they seemed right to me, to the exclusion of the million other directions I could have gone in.

We commonly think of the past as fixed and the future as undetermined, but when I work in the past it seems open, and when I ponder the future it seems closed. I'm not saying that the future *is* closed. (The suspicion that it is can be terrifying. I knew a student who was on the edge of madness while for six months he was sure that there would never be anything new under the sun, that there was nothing he could do that had not been done before.) In the 1990 motion picture, *Mr. Destiny,* Michael Caine plays a mysterious bartender who can create for you an alternative story of your life—"Oh, if I had just hit a home run in the last inning of the championship game instead of striking out!"—and shows you that if one little thing is changed, *everything* subsequent is different. No, I'm not talking about what past and future *are,* but how they *seem* when I think about them.

The émigré Czech novelist Milan Kundera indirectly confirms my intuition when he explains the political significance of past and future. "People are always shouting they want to create a better future. It's not true. The future is an apathetic void of no interest to anyone. The past is full of life, eager to irritate us, provoke and insult us, tempt us to destroy or repaint it. The only reason people want to be masters of the future is to change the past. They are fighting for access to the laboratories where photographs are retouched and biographies and histories rewritten." Kundera offers an unforgettable account of a retouched picture. At the moment in 1948 when Communist Czechoslovakia was born, the new leaders stood on a balcony in Prague to address the people. One of the officials, Clementis, took off his cap and put it on the head of another, Gottwald, to protect him from the snow. A photo of the event was widely distributed. "Every child knew the photograph from posters, schoolbooks, and museums." Four years later, Clementis was charged with treason and executed. The propaganda section excised him from the picture. "All that remains of Clementis is the cap on Gottwald's head."

Time cracks or crawls. The past makes me dizzy, the future gives me claustrophobia. There is yet a third reason for my "incompatible" sympathies for both the short view (the human story is nearly over) and the long view (we've only just begun): We do not know which is right. There is one prediction, however, that we have good reason to trust. In about five billion years the sun will have exhausted its nuclear fuel, and its remaining matter will expand enormously, engulfing the earth and much else besides. Some people who do not believe in God find this prospective conclusion to the story horrible. A few get round their despair by believing that long before the sun becomes a red giant, human beings will have devised ways to abandon planet earth and make their way to the vicinity of some younger, more hospitable star. I believe in God, *and* I, too, try to avoid thinking about the future of the earth as astrophysicists predict it. Christian friends who tell me that all this is irrelevant to the claims of the gospel puzzle me not because I distrust their sincerity but because I am unable to imagine how they insulate their theology from such speculations.

And there is a fourth reason: To refuse—or, better, to find myself unable—to come down on one side or other of the sooner/later divide prepares me to recognize the truth on both sides of what is often declared to be another incompatibility. Does history go in circles, or is it moving in a straight line? When I began to study the development of the biblical tradition, I was instructed that circular thought was characteristic of ancient Greece, and that the Bible introduced to the world the radically different concept of linear time—time going somewhere, with a purpose. To an undergraduate, eager for clear distinctions and unassailable conclusions, determined to make his way in the world, such clear-cut difference was immensely attractive, and the purported biblical option was clearly preferable.

In subsequent years, on the basis of more experience reinforced by the feminist critique of ways of thinking that had previously seemed "natural" to me, I have come to distrust neat distinctions, boxes labeled "either" and "or." Circular thinking, for which one of the classic expressions can be found in the Bible itself—"There is nothing new under the sun" (Ecclesiastes 1:9)—and linear thinking, characteristic of the prophets—"I am about to do a new thing," says the Lord (Isaiah 43:19)—are not necessarily incompatible.

History does not repeat itself but rhymes

Mark Twain is credited with the observation that history doesn't repeat itself but rhymes. As in poems, sometimes the rhymes are internal, sometimes they are in adjoining lines (lines that may be short or long), and sometimes they are in different verses. Stretches of free verse may intrude for a while. And a rhyme is not only a reminder of how something sounded in a previous line: when listening to a poem, we may try to guess what the coming rhyme will be.

The Bible itself is a great poem, in which the rhymes are not so much words as themes and patterns. When the prophets explained to the Israelites in the Babylonian Exile what had happened and where hope lurked in despair, they patterned their message on the already ancient story of the Exodus from Egypt. God would do something new, they said, but it would also be reassuringly familiar. In other words, history would rhyme. The early Christians found in the passage through the waters of the Red Sea an image for baptism. The story of an individual Christian's salvation, they believed, "rhymes" with the story of the deliverance of God's people in the time of Moses. In our own day, Latin American Christians have injected new life into theology by insisting that liberation from oppression (and even from the church's too easy alliance with political, military, and commercial power) is the divine theme with which their life must rhyme.

The Bible repeatedly replays ancient melodies transposed into a new key. This is entirely different from the confident claims of so many Christians today that they know exactly who or what fulfills a particular "prediction" in Daniel or Revelation. To say that history rhymes is to catch both the predictable and the unpredictable—the fundamental patterns that seem to repeat themselves but with manifold variations.

The late Samuel Sandmel, one of the wisest New Testament scholars of this century, was a rabbi. Because he was a careful historian, and also, perhaps, because he did not have the same religious stake in the New Testament as most of its interpreters, he maintained a clarity and even-handedness refreshing in a field where new methods rapidly breed new "certainties." After many years of patient poring over first-century sources and modern studies, Sandmel wrote:

> The more I work in that [first] century, the more persuaded I become that scholars have in significant part deceived themselves about the possibilities of exact and responsible conclusions. The bent among scholars seems to be that of

knowing more than can be known; they seem to be certain—where I find myself tantalized by uncertainties. Scholars very often seem to consider themselves able to solve problems which, perversely, remain continuing enigmas to me.

Sandmel refers to "the wish of the scholars to know more than could be known," and of course this is a wish hardly confined to scholars. All of us, at least sometimes, wish to know more than we can, and we need calm but steady reminders, from the likes of Rabbi Sandmel, that not to admit the limits of our knowledge is to appear rather foolish.

I am unable to say what "the" Christian view of time is, whether we are talking about when "long ago" was, what "now" is, or when the "then" of the return of Christ will be. I did not say I "refuse" to say these things, but that I am unable. My agnosticism about the Christian view of time used to make me ill at ease with those who are very sure of what it is, but now I can be comfortable with some who put things a way that I never would. If, however, someone tells me that I have to choose, that Christians cannot sit on the fence, blow hot and cold, function while holding two contradictory ideas at the same time, I simply say that I am unable to make that choice and find it unnecessary to do so. I cannot deny the shock delivered to my intellectual system by the slip of a finger that sprang me ahead to the 198th century. I cannot undo the way my encounter with Buddhist, Jewish, and Muslim calendars broadened my understanding of "now." I cannot rule out the conviction of either friend, one of whom says the story is nearly over, the other of whom says it has scarcely begun.

The cosmos and the carousel

In a period of sixteen months, between April 1988 and August 1989, I came the closest I have ever managed to making sense of time and its complex mystery.

It was one o'clock in the morning on April 2, 1988, Holy Saturday. Christ lay in the tomb. My second marriage, after fifteen good years, had recently been thrown into sudden disarray. Efforts at communication were blocked, like X-rays obstructed by the earth's atmosphere, or, like the shuttle *Challenger,* they exploded right after launch. I was reading *Perfect Symmetry: The Search for the Beginning of Time,* and was thinking in cosmic terms: three hundred million light years to neighboring galaxies; black holes with the mass of five billion suns; the enticing (though bizarre) fact that toward the center of the Milky Way there is enough vodka (a molecule at a time, alas) to fill ten thousand earth-size goblets.

I was awake in the middle of the night because my younger daughter, then almost ten, diagnosed a few months earlier with diabetes, had the flu and was vomiting. I imagined her pancreas as a shut-down white dwarf star. Her injected insulin had little to work on, and she would have blacked out if she couldn't keep some sugar in. Doctor's orders: a tablespoon of Seven-Up every twenty minutes. Memory-warp back to childhood, to my great-uncle who was our family physician when I was growing up. Seven-Up was often his prescription, and it worked wonders. But this was different. Seven-Up had merely settled my stomach. It was keeping Juliet from losing consciousness.

While spoon-feeding my daughter, I was overwhelmed by disparities of scale: The difference between the few inches I moved the spoon from the bottle to her lips and the distance that light traveled in the twenty minutes between doses: two hundred twenty-three million, five hundred twenty thousand, eight hundred miles. I actually calculated the distance right then.

When it was time for another tablespoon, the Seven-Up advertising tag popped into my head—"No caffeine: Never had it, Never will"—and triggered a temporal implosion. I thought: Never, forever, now, then, tomorrow. I felt that I could use an Easter.

The next day was Easter, but not the one I needed. The one I needed took nearly a year and a half to arrive, and it caught me entirely off guard, because I am not given to mystical experiences.

In August 1989 I bought a ticket and got on a carousel. I hadn't the slightest anticipation that following the ride I would know the world and time in a different way. I had already suspected that God is sneaky. After the ride on the merry-go-round, I knew it.

I had recently been rummaging through family papers, some more than a century old, and had found the dead coming to life in the words they had written when they were every bit as much alive as I was now. Time, in short, was already in flux when I stepped on the carousel.

Within a few turns I had an almost tactile (not visual) sense that God was suddenly there on the horse at my side. I was dizzy, but not from the kind of vertigo brought on by my amusement park nemesis, the Tilt-A-Whirl. I was seeing the universe whole and unbound. I was experiencing a moment in and out of time. The sensation was instantaneous, and yet it seemed eternal. The carousel took me through time and through space. During the four or five minutes of the ride all time twisted up tight and all the galaxies gathered in those few yards of radius.

Mystical experiences unattached to the rest of one's life may be of interest, but they are of little use. The test of a mystical experience is always: What next? The carousel stopped, and I got off onto the world that I had gotten on from. What did it mean for me to have sat briefly next to God on a rusty carousel?

Nobody, myself included, expected me to have a direct experience of God. Anybody, myself included, might have expected the consequence of the experience to be dramatic. But the aftermath was quiet and gave me a new understanding of something a monk friend of mine said. He noted that many people assume he must have regular access to God's immediate presence. When they ask him where he looks for God, he has a disconcerting response. They expect some esoteric answer that they can ponder and marvel at for a while, and their faces fall when he says, simply, "I go to church." Basically, that's the implication I found in the carousel ride: mostly to keep eating bread and drinking wine, that is, to continue participating in the ritual and communal life of the church. But there was more. I had a new appreciation of God's intimate presence in and to the world, and I could now read past, present, and future as the story of rides on God's carousel. By turning, turning, we may come round right, as the old Shaker hymn has it. With the carousel's motion still a recent memory, the Easter I needed came to me in the six-hundred-year-old words of Dame Julian of Norwich, as fresh as tomorrow: "And all shall be well, and all shall be well, and all manner of thing shall be well." Dame Julian lived long before carousel rides, but her words, with their repetition and their gradually slowing cadence, capture perfectly the difficult-to-express turning to eternity that I experienced on that August day.

Ever since reading Saint Gregory the Great's account of Saint Benedict's sixth-century vision, I had been intrigued and baffled—and, truth to tell, envious:

> According to his own description, the whole world was gathered up before his eyes in what appeared to be a single ray of light. . . . Of course, in saying that the world was gathered up before his eyes I do not mean that heaven and earth grew small, but that his spirit was enlarged. Absorbed as he was in God, it was now easy for him to see all that lay beneath God.

In April 1988, while I fed my sick daughter Seven-Up early in the morning on Holy Saturday, light-years and "never, forever, now, then, tomorrow" gaped menacingly, no "single ray of light" but a dimensionless darkness, Christ in bonds of death. On the carousel in August 1989, without regard for the details of the liturgical calendar, my plea for an Easter was answered. The centuries were linked, networked, webbed, and into all of this was woven my own family history, the century-old letters I had been reading shortly before I hopped on the wooden horse. My spirit was enlarged. Bafflement gave way to amazement, envy to experience.

"Cantata for Resolution of a Paradox"

In 1979, the imagination of two of my students provided an unexpected resource for reaching the equilibrium of being able to hold two opposed ideas in the mind at the same time. Phillip Kloeckner and John McKinstry, sophomores in "Introduction to the New Testament," found that they could not answer, on the basis of the biblical text itself, the question of whether salvation is by faith or by works. The syllabus offered the option of a creative project in place of a traditional term paper, and Kloeckner and McKinstry, capable musicians, chose several "salvation by faith" passages and several that promote "salvation by works," and wrote "Cantata for Resolution of a Paradox." The individual movements are clever and give musical expression to the contrasting ideas. But the stroke of genius is the piece's conclusion: It fashions the paradox into a double fugue, a musical double helix in which both faith and works twist and spiral, imitate and counterpoint each other, so that musically they are inextricable one from the other. The score resolves the faith/works problem by dissolving it in a cascade of sound.

Some of the composers' friends performed "Cantata for

Resolution of a Paradox," and I played the tape for the class at the end of the final examination. That moment has ever since signaled for me the power unfettered imagination possesses to spring open the intellectual and spiritual traps that we think we are caught in. Christ coming tomorrow? Christ coming in a million years? We need musicians to compose a cantata for that one—or playwrights, poets, painters, novelists. The only trouble with depending on imagination to "retain the ability to function" while holding onto contradictory ideas is that you can never predict where the imaginative light is going to shine from, or even that it will shine when you need it to.

But such uncertainty leads to theological clarity. The Book of Daniel tells the story of three Israelites—Shadrach, Meshach, and Abednego—who refuse to obey the decree of King Nebuchadnezzar of Babylon that everyone in his realm fall down and worship the golden statue he has made. The king threatens to throw them into a fiery furnace and mocks them: "Who is the god that will deliver you out of my hands?" The three men give an answer that acknowledges the terms set by the king: "O Nebuchadnezzar, we have no need to present a defense to you in this matter. If our God whom we serve is able to deliver us from the furnace of blazing fire and out of your hand, O king, let him deliver us." Thus far the terms make sense to the monarch: Even if you are a god, they say to Nebuchadnezzar, our God can beat you up. However, Shadrach, Meshach, and Abednego have more to say: "But if not, be it known to you, O king, that we will not serve your gods and we will not worship the golden statue that you have set up" (Daniel 3:15–18). In other words, our devotion to our God is not dependent on his exercise of power on our behalf.

The three men saw God, not the projections of their desires, not their longing for security, not their eagerness to bash the Babylonians, but the God they determined to be worthy of worship because God is God, not because God is at their beck and call, bound to their timetable or their convictions about "sooner" or "later." Despite their uncertainty as to the way in which God would respond to their plight, the three Israelites saw God in the clarity of their commitment; their own wishes did not get in the way.

Jonathan Edwards, in eighteenth-century Connecticut, far in time and space from the Babylon of Nebuchadnezzar, was one in spirit with Shadrach, Meshach, and Abednego. Edwards was theologically and philosophically a committed Calvinist, strongly convinced of predestination. The power of God was absolute and largely inscrutable. From such a starting point it would be easy to despair, or to abandon all limits. But here are two entries from Edwards's "Resolutions." They were written three days apart, when he was nineteen, in the year that he received his M.A. from Yale.

50. *Resolved,* That I will act so, as I think I shall judge would have been best, and most prudent, when I come into the future world. July 5, 1723.

51. *Resolved,* That I will act so, in every respect, as I think I shall wish I had done, if I should at last be damned. July 8, 1723.

I first read these two statements more than thirty years ago. Their mesmerizing effect was like the astonishment I would know later when my finger slipped on the typewriter. These two resolutions come to *exactly the same thing.* How Edwards would try to live was quite without regard for whether he would be spending eternity in heaven or hell. His trust in God, his commitment and loyalty, lay far deeper than the question "What happens when I die?" For Shadrach, Meshach, and Abednego, and for me in those rare moments when I am being faithful to the grace that has found me, the answer to "When is it?" is not a calculation on a calendar but a pledge, expressed in another of Edwards's "Resolutions": "6. *Resolved,* To live with all my might, while I do live."

ON WHERE WE ARE

The "Morning Show" on Minnesota Public Radio, which I listen to while driving to work, often plays songs by request. One that gets asked for repeatedly is Monty Python's "Galaxy Song." Designed to lift your spirit when life is pressing it down, the song locates us on a planet that revolves nine hundred miles an hour, orbiting the sun at nineteen miles a second, and moving a million miles a day. The cosmological juggernaut plunges on into the hundred billion stars of the Milky Way, and finally carries us among the billions upon billions of galaxies. The song is lighthearted, but a vein of anxiety laced through the humor accounts for the song's steady popularity. Though I hesitate to come right out and say what Pascal exclaimed three centuries ago—"the eternal silence of these infinite spaces terrifies me"—I recognize that Pascal has given voice to my own fears.

Too cramped or too vast

"Where are we?" The question is haunting, in part because it is so easy to feel totally imprisoned, stuck, immobile, like the characters Nagg and Nell who spend all of Samuel Beckett's play *Endgame* in two adjacent trash cans, or to feel totally lost in a vast expanse without boundaries. Kevin Kling wrote a play that portrays the life of the Seven Dwarfs after Snow White departs with the prince. One of the dwarfs, Dave, leaves their home in the woods to search for news of Snow White. He travels through a barren wasteland, represented on the stage by two huge pure white sheets, one as the ground, one billowing as the sky. There are no lines, no limits, there is no horizon. "I wonder how far I've gone," he says. "It's good to be out here. At night, in the dark, alone, by myself. What was that? Just the wind. Just the wind or the snakebear. Or worse maybe it's my imagination. Then it could be anything." When I heard these lines I thought of the times I had "reassured" my kids that the monster under the bed was "just your imagination"—and thereby multiplied their fear, for "then it could be anything."

Whether we identify with Beckett's Nagg and Nell stuck in trash cans, our spirits confined, crushed, or with Kling's dwarf Dave, literally scared out of our wits, our spirits dissipating into the void—or more likely, if some days we feel that space is too cramped and some days too vast—the question, Where are we? cannot be avoided.

There is certainly no one Christian answer to the question, Where are we? The Bible and church tradition offer many images—God's footstool, a vale of tears, the devil's playground, a garden of delights, a field of wheat blighted with weeds, a school, a prison, a pilgrimage route, a proving ground, to name just a few. Some people, finding the world falling drastically short of the perfection they would have created had the job been theirs, have denounced the world in the name of Christ. This view was already in vogue in the second century, when Marcion, who was excommunicated by a bishop (his father), claimed that Jesus came "from that Father who is above the god that made the world." In other words, where we are is precisely where we should not be, and Christ came to spring us free from the trap.

For the vast majority of Christians, however, both in the past and now, there is no doubt that we belong here, even if from time to time we want to shout, "Stop the world, I want to get off!" But for us, in a way more insistent than for persons in earlier ages, puzzles about the nature of this place where we are and where we belong abound. In earlier eras, it was easier to imagine stopping the world. Indeed, it was already stopped. The earth was stable and stationary at the center, and fixed spheres moved around it.

But then Copernicus placed the sun at the center. Galileo found moons where theory and theology were sure they shouldn't be. Telescopes and satellites and mathematics have taught us how tiny the earth is, and how young; how small the solar system is in the Milky Way; how infinitesimal the Milky Way in the immense spaces that terrified Pascal. The Hubble

Space Telescope has quintupled the number of galaxies that we know about, from around ten billion to around fifty billion. Absolute space and absolute time, which provided fixed reference points for physics, for imagination, and for prayer, were wiped away by Einstein.

Everything moves

The most drastic change in thought, feeling, and attitude that has occurred between all earlier centuries and our own is our inescapable conviction that everything is in motion and that everything undergoes change. Even when it became clear, with Newton, that everything was moving, there was still the comforting assumption that in the realm of the heavens what stars were, are, and will be, remained forever the same. We now know that the heavens are violent beyond imagining, that stars are born, live, and die, displaying beauty and wreaking havoc on a scale that is, quite literally, cosmic. In a note to Einstein, the publicity director of the Metropolitan Opera wrote, "Relativity: There is no hitching post in the universe—so far as we know," and Einstein penned, "Read, and found correct."

And just in the past two decades the last vestige of feeling that *terra* is really *firma,* that we have, if only in a very narrow compass, a fixed place to stand, has been compromised by the science of plate tectonics: The continents are skating across the mantle of the earth.

But not even this is the full extent of the assault on our sensibilities, for physicists and mathematicians are now proposing that the world is organized according to the principles of chaos theory (or better, complexity theory), making it impossible to extrapolate to future states of anything, including the universe itself, from even the most theoretically complete information.

To think about where we are—a universe in which everything, *everything*, is moving, decaying, changing, and finally unpredictable—can seem a spiritual roller-coaster ride.

And the cosmological and the political are of a piece. Future historians, trying to account for our era, will gravitate, I suspect, to the story of Sergei Krikalev, the cosmonaut who rocketed to the Soviet space station on May 18, 1991, and returned to the independent state of Kazakhstan on March 25, 1992. As the Associated Press dispatch noted in a sentence that has a liturgical compression and rhythm, "While Krikalev was in space, Communist governments toppled throughout Eastern Europe, his old country ceased to exist, his hometown of Leningrad was renamed St. Petersburg, and the once-proud Soviet space program had to turn to the West for money." During the ten months in which Krikalev orbited the planet, the world he left had changed beyond recognition.

The more I read about cosmology (and, indeed, about politics), the more I am persuaded that Lewis Carroll is the most faithful guide we have to the world we live in. As Alice remarks, things get "curiouser and curiouser," less and less commonsensical. Every new discovery takes us down the hole to Wonderland once more. The physicist Wolfgang Pauli, after presenting a paper on elementary particles, turned to his colleague Niels Bohr and said, "You probably think these ideas are crazy." Bohr replied, "I do, but unfortunately they are not crazy enough." Lewis Carroll's White Queen, who could imagine six impossible things before breakfast, would probably ace a physics quiz at Caltech. Carroll was both a mathematician and a cleric (he was ordained a deacon in the Church of England), and he liked to make up stories for children—three traits that in combination compose as clear-eyed and level-headed a perspective as we are ever apt to get on where we are.

But Carroll is well known. Edwin Abbott (1838–1926), six years Carroll's junior and his distinct inferior as a writer, was in his own way equally adept as a teaser of the imagination. Abbott has helped my imagination turn Tilt-A-Whirl frenzy into the more measured movement of a carousel.

Flatland

Many people think that people used to think that the earth is flat. I remember dramatic grade-school accounts of Christopher Columbus trying to persuade a skeptical court that supporting his voyage would not be throwing their money over the edge of the world. But Daniel J. Boorstin, in *The Discoverer,* has demonstrated that there is little evidence that many people at any time, including Columbus, believed the earth to be flat. Edwin Abbott, however, asks, "What if the world *were* flat?" and he does not mean flat simply as "not round." He means really flat: just two dimensions, length and breadth.

Abbott's *Flatland* is an account of life in such a world, especially of the bafflement that would confound the inhabitants if a three-dimensional character were to appear among them. They would have no way to experience, no way to perceive, not even any way really to imagine what a solid would be like. If a sphere were to pass through their world, for instance, it would appear first as a dot, then as an expanding circle that would reach a maximum circumference and start retracting until it once again was reduced to a dot. Then it would vanish. The Flatlanders couldn't look up to see the sphere coming, because in Flatland there is no "up." Flatland is not Wonderland, and Abbott is not a world-class literary genius. But *Flatland* deeply altered the way I think and feel about our three-dimensional world.

Dimension-talk these days quickly escalates into esoteric realms that make the contrast between Flatland and the world of our experience seem so elementary as to be comic. Now and then I have fleeting moments of thinking that maybe I have an inkling of what Einstein meant by time being a fourth dimension. But even if I were to manage four dimensions, I am left far behind. Some very bright cosmologists are theorizing that in the early universe there were twenty-six dimensions, and all but four of them are now tied up in bundles infinitesimally small. Would Abbott's point be the same had he written a book about a twenty-six-dimensional character trying to communicate with inhabitants of a twenty-five-dimensional world? And what does it mean for my sense of where I am that astrophysicist Adam Frank uses the geometry of 60,000-dimensional cigars to understand globular clusters? I do not know.

I hope that someone in the line of Carroll and Abbott will emerge in our own time to help us glimpse what the cosmologists see while acknowledging the boundaries beyond which our imaginations cannot yet go. Mathematicians, to hear them tell it, go to other dimensions as routinely as they take a taxi across town. Travel to the fifth, seventh, tenth, twenty-sixth dimension is "nothing special," says Albert Marden of the Geometry Center in Minneapolis. "To a mathematician, it's an everyday event." Such journeys are certainly no everyday event for me, though when I read that "to a mathematician, a dimension is a degree of freedom," I'm eager to take the trip. For now, however, we can look to Abbott, who portrays a world of reduced dimensions, for help in thinking about a world where dimensions are proliferating. *Flatland* raises fundamental questions about what we take for granted.

Abbott does not hide the religious implications of his book. The Sphere that appears in Flatland as an expanding and contracting Circle has a mission: to preach the Gospel of Three Dimensions. Flatlanders have legends of enchanters and magicians who darkly hinted at realms beyond imagining—and were eliminated from the community as dangerous traitors. Even in Flatland, prophets are without honor in their own country. Theological terms like "manifestation," "revelation," "vision," and "evangelization" crop up repeatedly in the book. From the perspective of Flatlanders, the Sphere seems to enter closed rooms, reminding alert readers of the stories of Jesus' appearances after the resurrection. The Flatlander who is taken by the Sphere above the plane of Flatland and introduced to the mysteries of the Land of Three Dimensions has trouble remembering what was seen, like mystics who have difficulty expressing what they have experienced, or like Paul who reports that he was "caught up to the third heaven" and "heard things that cannot be told" (2 Corinthians 12:2–4).

At the beginning of *Flatland,* Abbott, or rather, "A Square" (the Flatlander who is the supposed author), suggests the fundamental motive for writing the book. After describing the geography and inhabitants of Flatland, the Square says that the reader now has "a pretty correct notion of my country and countrymen. Alas, a few years ago, I should have said 'my universe'; but now my mind has been opened to higher views of things." "Alas" signals a bittersweet truth: The "higher views" are both exhilaration and torment. Writing from prison, where he has been confined as punishment for his brash attempt to alert his fellow citizens to the reality of the world of spheres and cubes, the Square explains why he has bothered writing at all: "I exist in the hope that these memoirs, in some manner, I know not how, may find their way to the minds of humanity in Some Dimension, and may stir up a new race of rebels who shall refuse to be confined to limited Dimensionality."

Between "never" and "we know all about it"

Prior to the eighteenth century, the Christian imagination was not straitjacketed by "limited Dimensionality." The reality of unseen realms (the Nicene Creed credits God as Maker of all things visible *and invisible*) was assumed, and while there was always the danger that an unanticipated and unexplainable happening was sinister and menacing, a device of malevolent forces, such an occurrence might be a breakthrough from an unseen realm, like the Sphere appearing as a point and then as an expanding and contracting circle in Flatland. We have inherited from our more immediate ancestry a suspicion, amounting to a dogma, that what we see is what we've got, and there is nothing more. Theology has taken a strident this-worldly turn.

Such a turn needed to be taken. For centuries, theology had been caught in a spirit/matter, heaven/earth dualism, and to say that faith has to do only with what is beyond the world and beyond this life is a travesty in a tradition that says God came into the world and is fully present here. Follow the dualistic road for a while, and you arrive at the chilling remark I once heard attributed to the nineteenth-century German Chancellor, Bismarck, "I believe in an afterlife, therefore I do not take human life terribly seriously." However, in the interests of eliminating the sharp distinction between flesh and spirit, recent theologians have too often discarded the spirit altogether. We might learn from Abbott's book, which insists that the realm beyond is not in some different universe, remote from the here and now, an escape from the world we know, but is part of the reality that surrounds us, in which we are embedded. Our problem is not what the psychological and social critics of Christianity have chided us for: that we make up dream worlds in order to compensate for a miserable existence that is, in Hobbes's phrase, "solitary, poor, nasty, brutish, and short." Our problem is that we have let these critics cut the nerve of our imaginations so that we can no longer recognize the messages, the intimations, that cut across our world like expanding circles in Flatland. Like the Square, we assume that the circle cannot be telling us of anything beyond itself.

By no means do I advocate accepting every claim to special revelation made by every rebel who refuses to be confined to limited Dimensionality. There are lots of crazy people, and the untutored imagination can run wild. But avoiding gullibility does not require me to say that there is nothing I will swallow. In the preface to the second edition of *Flatland,* Edwin Abbott measures with precision the middle ground that the Christian imagination has sadly abandoned. The book is designed, he says, to "prove suggestive as well as amusing, to those Space-landers of moderate and modest minds who—speaking of that which is of the highest importance, but lies beyond experience—decline to say on the one hand, 'This can never be,' and on the other hand, 'It must needs be precisely thus, and we know all about it.'" There is a great deal of territory between "never" and "we know all about it." This territory "between" is an ironic Christian's natural habitat.

It is a territory that needs to be reclaimed. It has been en-
croached on for over a century since Friedrich Nietzsche's
bold declaration, in 1882, that "God is dead." God's terminal
illness had been suspected and rumored for a long time before
Nietzsche delivered the coroner's report. The nineteenth century's suspicion that God was sick, and its conviction finally
that God was dead, was quite different from the eighteenth
century's suspicion that there probably wasn't any God at all,
or if there was one, there was no need to bother or worry,
since the world God had created was a well-oiled machine,
working on its own. The eighteenth century saw the eclipse of
God as the dawning of a bright new day; it felt the burden of
God being lifted off its shoulders. The nineteenth century,
haunted by what Matthew Arnold called the "melancholy,
long withdrawing roar" of the ebbing sea of faith, felt the
ground of God washing away beneath its feet.

Nietzsche, to be sure, shed no tears at God's funeral. He ex-
ulted in the death of the tyrant, and though he recognized that
"some sun seems to have set just now," he declared that for the
elite the consequences were "not at all sad and dark, but rather
like a new, scarcely describable kind of light, happiness, relief,
exhilaration, encouragement, dawn." The sea, which had
brought melancholy to Arnold two decades earlier, became for
Nietzsche an image of new possibility: "At last the horizon
appears free again to us, even granted that it is not bright; at
last our ships may venture out again, venture out to face any
danger; all the daring of the lover of knowledge is permitted
again; the sea, *our* sea, lies open again; perhaps there has never
yet been such an 'open sea.'"

In the intervening century the open sea of possibility upon which Nietzsche gazed has narrowed into a kind of Bermuda Triangle into which the hopes and confident expectations of the late nineteenth and early twentieth centuries have disappeared. The modern world has dismally failed to live up to its advance billing. No other century has been littered with so many corpses as ours. But we are beginning to wake from our stupor. It is very late, though maybe not too late. W. H. Auden speaks for us: "We who must die demand a miracle."

Miracle and surprise

A miracle." An outdated, outmoded, discredited word. As Edwin Abbott suspected, the first symptom of God's eventual death was the atrophy and degeneration of miracle, beginning in the seventeenth century with the ascendency of mechanical explanation. The world became a flatland, a closed system, rudely inhospitable to the unexpected, and God was expected to operate strictly within the bounds of the possible. Surprise was peremptorily ruled out of court.

I don't claim ever to have been party to a clear-cut miracle, but I do know that a precondition for recognizing one if it happens is openness to surprise. I get a lot of help from Edwin Abbott and a host of modern-day scientists who uncover a most curious universe. James Bryant Conant, chemist and president of Harvard University, said that after sustaining the shock of Einstein's theory of relativity, which dismantled the whole scheme of physical reality on which the nineteenth century's science had been based, he could never again consider any theory about the physical world to be the last word.

Roland M. Frye, a noted critic of English literature, registers the significance of this shift for fields far beyond the scientific. He identifies "the basic delusion inherited from our immediate past [as] the assurance that it is possible to define truth completely in all its aspects, to formulate it in statements and equations." He goes on to document "a narrowing of focus, a simplification of understanding, a foreshortening of the human vision" in a whole array of human endeavors. But Frye sees this unfortunate legacy from the past three centuries as itself eroding, clearing the way for the return of an "as if" world. "There are shifts in the ways of looking and seeing in science and indeed everywhere else. . . . Wherever we look, we encounter a growing recognition of pervasive mystery, of the limits of our ability to define, to delineate, to compress reality into neat packages. We live again in a world of awe, a world of hypotheses, of the 'as if' and not of the 'just like.' "

The world of "as if," the space "between" that I want to reclaim and reoccupy, is available to Christians today in a way and to a degree unknown to our ancestors just a few generations ago. But a surprising world will surprise us only if we let it. Learning how to be surprised is a tough spiritual discipline, requiring me to unlearn habits long formed and hard caked. I must value what I have been taught to dismiss as naive and be prepared to recognize what is out of date as the latest thing. I have to give up what C. S. Lewis calls "chronological snobbery," the self-satisfied and self-gratifying judgment that every-thing earlier is necessarily inferior.

Becoming a born-again reader

When I was an undergraduate I heard a story about Pro-fessor B. J. Whiting, Harvard's Chaucer expert, whose heart was warm but whose exterior was crusty. A doctoral stu-dent came to him in an acute state of fluster and asked, "What can I do to prepare for my Ph.D. exams?" Professor Whiting's answer was brief and pointed: "Read." In my experience, that could just as well be the answer to my question, "What can I do to get ready to be surprised?"

At the beginning of my introductory Bible courses I said to my students that those unfamiliar with the text should not consider themselves at a disadvantage. Indeed, I envied them, because I could never read the Bible as an adult as if I had not known it from childhood. I asked those to whom it was fresh to tell me what it is like to *discover* it. One student came to me two weeks into the semester in near despair. "I've been look-ing everywhere for the footnotes and can't find them." The only superscript numbers he had previously seen in books were footnote references, so he naturally thought that there must be one for every numbered verse. Not all reports of first encounters were quite this basic, but from my students I learned how easy it is to let what I think of as sophistication insinuate itself between me and the text.

As a teacher, I was usually pretty good at getting and holding class attention, but one semester, about ten years into my teaching career, something wasn't working. I could sense resistance, even resentment, permeating the room. I asked some of the students to come see me. "What's wrong?" I asked. Their answer startled me: "You say to us, 'As I was preparing this lecture on Jeremiah for today, I noticed for the first time that. . . .' You need to remember that we haven't yet seen what you saw the *first* time." What I intended as a benefit to them—my remaining excited and engaged, even surprised by things I had been over many times—left them in the open sea without compass or sextant. I learned in that moment that the teacher's task is to encounter the material every time as if for the first time. Initial surprise has to be repeated, over and over again.

How can reading be continually surprising? I get help in answering this question from my friend Harry Nielsen. He is a philosopher, so he is well aware of the puzzles in reading: Is what the author really "meant" accessible to us? How much of our own bias do we inevitably impose on a piece of writing? Can words ever be pinned down? He is also, however, suspicious of the academic habit of multiplying difficulties beyond necessity. Our efforts to appear sophisticated he calls a form of evasion, a complicated kind of balk. We drag the heavy equipment of literary theory up to a work and try to force it to talk. The work is on trial, and goes silent.

As an alternative to this academic, professional way of reading, Nielsen advocates what he calls conversational reading. When I engage in conversation with a friend, I do not run what we both say through a maze of sociological and psychological theory. I may have a pretty good idea of what my friend will say, but if I have prejudged what my friend can mean, I can easily miss the new, the fresh, the unexpected. We never know the full context of what anybody says, even those with whom we are most intimate, and of course we bring our own prejudices to any interchange. But despite the fog and the signals both mixed and missed, we learn from each other, we surprise each other. We are not caught in a trap of our own devising or paralyzed by an inoculation of theory. And the same is true of reading. Nielsen makes a distinction between reading the way we read private letters and the way we read those addressed to "Occupant." When I engage the voice on the page in conversation, the way I would talk with a friend, I am treating the author as a companion, not as a specimen.

Curiously—or maybe not so curiously—academic training infects conversation itself so that surprise, even change, gets muted, stifled. The characteristic mode of a seminar or faculty meeting is this: The presenter strives to be so brilliant as to forestall criticism, while the listeners lie in wait for the weak points in the presenter's argument so that they can pounce and show their superiority, thus avoiding any challenge that the speaker might have addressed to their favorite prejudices. I was just as guilty as anyone. After faculty meetings, I found that I often meditated more on the clever things I'd said than on the provocative ideas of others.

Even if we want surprises, we want *predictable* surprises. Why else did so many students come to me at registration time and say, "Tell me exactly what your course is about, what I will be expected to do, what I will learn from it"? Nietzsche thought that the death of God heralded a new age of adventure and discovery. What we have instead is a squirreling away into professionalisms and specializations, and discovery falls prey to defensiveness. Curiosity, which presupposes real conversation, a willingness, in the wise words of Folly as Erasmus reports them, "to make mistakes together or individually . . . [and] wisely overlook things," can make no headway against our worship of expertise and our obsession with always being right.

God died because people forgot how to read. With a sharp irony, the Bible was pinched between two forgettings. From one side the Bible was—and is in many quarters today—treated as so sacred as to be dictated word for word by God so that the Bible is totally unlike anything else we read. From the other side, the Bible was—and is in many quarters today—subjected to heavy interpretive equipment, and like other writing the Bible gets shielded from the clear light of that original and most wonderful of a child's requests, "Read me a story." When the life is squeezed out of the Bible, from whatever direction, when the Bible is exiled from "the space between" into the extremes of "we know all about it" or "this can never be," the living God can no longer be found there.

Once I learned the answer "conversationally" to the question, "How can I read?" I had to wonder: "How can I, who know only professional reading, become again like a child? How can I be born again—that is, become a *born-again reader?*" It has not been easy. I have had to abandon a pride I justified as academic rigor. I must now prepare myself for the text, the words themselves, to shatter my treasured theories and schemes, though I am accustomed after all these years to see whatever piece of writing I am attacking at the moment as if it were in a courtroom dock being cross-examined by these very theories and schemes. The discipline of reading is much like a *New Yorker* review's praise of a book: The author's "charm is due to his attentiveness, his ability to be still and observe something unfold without interrupting." I have been carefully trained to be an interrupter.

To recognize the God of surprises, who is the God of the Bible and the creator of this amazing and expanding universe where we are, who interrupts *us,* we do not need a new hermeneutical theory—that is, a theory of interpretation that will tell us what are and are not legitimate ways to read. We need a new sensibility, a rebirth of imagination, a loosening up of stiff spiritual joints. We in the West need to look East and go back to the future.

Icons help us read the world

More than a millennium ago a debate about icons split the church. For a century—four generations—Christians argued, went to jail, excommunicated one another, and spent years in exile because they disagreed about the role of pictures in worship. Ever since the year 843, when icons were officially restored, the Orthodox Church, which we classify as "Eastern," though there are millions of its followers in the West, has celebrated annually the Triumph of Orthodoxy. What historians call the Iconoclastic Controversy takes up very little room in the consciousness of most Western Christians, who, if they are aware of such a dispute at all, think not of eighth-century Byzantium but of sixteenth-century Reformation shock troops smashing statues and slashing paintings.

Western Christians these days don't regularly destroy images, but we are subliminally suspicious of them. Many Protestants were taught by John Calvin, who said of the Orthodox teaching on icons, "so disgusting are their absurdities that I am ashamed even to mention them," and the Catholic Church, which has often appeared to Protestant eyes a hotbed of idolatry, was uneasy with the Orthodox position even at the time of the Iconoclastic Controversy itself. This may all seem quite remote from here and now, but Orthodox icons are the best clue we have as to where we are. They can help us read the world.

When I enter the Byzantine section of an art museum and gaze reverently at the icons on the walls, I may think that I am experiencing what the Orthodox experience when they enter a church, but I am not. Tutored in Western assumptions about artistic creativity, I am marveling at the beauty fashioned long ago by someone, probably someone anonymous. I may ponder the view of the world reflected in the icon, a view different from my own, but the object before my eyes teases me into thoughts about the artist who saw the world that way. I feel myself in the presence of genius, not in the forecourts of heaven.

For the Orthodox, the icon is a window, but not one through which we gaze into the divine realm. Rather, it is a window through which the inhabitants of that realm—Christ, the angels, the saints—are looking at us. This distinction explains one of the characteristic, and decidedly non-Western, features of icons: their reverse, or inverse, perspective. Ever since the Renaissance, Western painting has created perspective by locating the vanishing point within a picture. This way of portraying the world is so commonplace, so familiar, that it seems to us "natural," "obvious." But the icon constructs perspective so that the vanishing point is *in front of* the picture; indeed, there are often multiple vanishing points, and the many lines of movement are *from* the icon *toward* the worshiper. The icon cracks through limited Dimensionality by coming to *you* instead of you coming to *it*. It encompasses you. And to the Orthodox this seems natural, obvious. After her journey to the center of the galaxy, radio astronomer Ellie Arroway, heroine of Carl Sagan's novel *Contact,* would understand what happens when an Orthodox Christian enters the door of a church filled with icons. That church door—to all appearances an ordinary door—is like the door through which Ellie's companions had stepped into another realm. Icons make perfect sense in the cosmos that Sagan and other scientists are unfolding for us.

The Iconoclastic Controversy, like every religious dispute, sucked into its vortex politics and economics, revenge, class conflict, ethnic rivalry, mistranslations, and occasional acts of selflessness and heroism. Figuring out what was really going on requires scholarly sleuthing that will never finally be done. Beneath all the mayhem, however, lay a fundamental disagreement about dimensions. The Iconoclasts, those who wanted to outlaw images in Christian worship, were, in Edwin Abbott's terms, "confined to limited Dimensionality." They wanted God to stay where they believed that God belonged, in an abstract realm that we can access only through thought untainted by the senses. The Iconoclasts were suspicious of the human capacity for idolatry, a well-warranted suspicion. But they were like the inhabitants of Flatland: unable to imagine that another dimension might intersect with their familiar surroundings. They "knew all about" what could "never happen."

From the Iconoclast perspective, the whole point of Christian revelation is to move beyond an infantile dependence on things and into pure spirit. According to Iconoclast belief, aids to worship are really impediments for the religiously proficient, and we can be assured of our kinship with God only insofar as we leave our humanity behind. Against this "logical" position, the Iconodules, those who favored the use of icons in Christian worship, argued that while *we* might judge such abstraction from the messy material world to be appropriate for God, God has chosen to operate differently. As one of my students once said, if God had wanted to appeal directly to our minds, Mary would have written a book instead of bearing a child.

A leading Iconodule, Saint John of Damascus, after compiling a catalogue of specific places such as Mount Sinai, Nazareth, and the Garden of Gethsemane, and material objects such as the manger, the swaddling clothes, and the wood of the cross, and much more besides, to make the case that God has chosen to come to the world through matter, says, "These and other such things I honor and worship, along with every holy sanctuary of God and everything over which God is named, not because of their own nature, but because they are vessels of divine energy, and it pleased God through them and in them to fashion our salvation." All these particularities, John realizes, are offensive to the Iconoclasts, and he chastises them, cramped by their limited Dimensionality, for pretending to know better than God knows what it is fitting for God to do and where it is fitting for God to be. Another Iconodule, Saint Theodore of Studios, further extends the range of John's argument: "Is there anywhere, among rational or irrational, animate or inanimate being, where divinity is not found?"

We Christians in the West characteristically wonder whether there is anywhere in the world that divinity *is* found. The default setting is God's absence. We may acknowledge that God speaks from time to time, and the incarnation assures us that God's absence isn't total, but we tend to relegate the reality of the incarnation to a period of about thirty-three years two millennia ago. We have the tradition of the *Imitation of Christ,* to be sure, and these days millions of people, when faced with a decision, are asking themselves, "What Would Jesus Do?" But deep within Western Christian sensibilities is the conviction that God is *wholly* other. When we repent (the root meaning of the New Testament Greek term translated "repent" is "turn around"), we find that we are facing a God whose ways are utterly different from ours, whom we have grievously offended.

Orthodox Christians, their spirituality formed in churches filled with icons that pulse with divine energy, see a different prospect when they repent, or turn around. For them, the default setting is God's presence: "Is there anywhere divinity is *not* found?" They find that they are facing a God whose ways are not so unlike their own. God is not challenging them to acknowledge their creatureliness, but is inviting them to discover their kinship to the divine. The classic statement is that of the fourth-century bishop of Alexandria, Saint Athanasius: Christ became what we are in order that we might become what he is. The Orthodox Christian does not have divine pretensions; he or she does not think "I'm going to become God." But the Orthodox Christian does believe that it is possible to share in the divine life, that the chasm between us and God is bridgeable.

From an Orthodox point of view, Saint Benedict's vision—when "the whole world was gathered up before his eyes in what appeared to be a single ray of light," and, "absorbed as he was in God, it was now easy for him to see all that lay beneath God"—would not be surprising at all. The reverse perspective of icons shakes the worshiper loose from limited Dimensionality. As a modern Orthodox theologian has put it, "The constructive role [of the icon] does not lie only in the teaching of the truths of the Christian faith, but in the education of the entire [human being, and] the goal of the icon is neither to provoke nor to exalt a natural human feeling. Its goal is to orient all our feelings, as well as our intellect and all the other aspects of our nature, towards the transfiguration."

This reference to the transfiguration signals the most profound Orthodox challenge to our Western Christian assumptions about where we are. The Orthodox certainly do not minimize the significance of the crucifixion; but while we in the West characteristically look to Golgotha, the hill of the three crosses outside Jerusalem, to see God most intensely present in the world, Eastern Christians characteristically look to

Mount Tabor, the traditional site of the transfiguration of Jesus, as the place where the reality of God most stunningly breaks into our limited Dimensionality: "Six days later, Jesus took with him Peter and James and his brother John and led them up a high mountain, by themselves. And he was transfigured before them, and his face shone like the sun, and his clothes became dazzling white" (Matthew 17:1–2). To the extent that we Western Christians pay any attention at all to the transfiguration (I recall hearing very few sermons on it), we treat it as a misplaced resurrection appearance, or as pointing to the transformation of the world at the return of Christ, but not as telling us something about the condition of the world here and now. We clam up when the holy in our midst hints that our Dimensionality is limited.

Shells on the shore of eternity

Not long ago I was taught a way to read the world in light of the transfiguration. One of my professional responsibilities is to take notes on discussions at the institute where I work. Thanks to the computer, I can type the notes directly into memory so that all I have to do is spell check and edit, avoiding the time-consuming and spirit-taxing middle term of transcribing. Participants in the consultations get used to the clicking of the keys, so used to it, in fact, that when I pause or cease typing, everyone notices.

A participant in one of our consultations is a professional imagist—she creates images with paint, with words, with objects of all sorts. When she starts to talk, everyone else in the group notices that the computer clicks become more hesitant, the pauses more frequent, and finally technological silence descends as my fingers admit they cannot do justice to Casey Flynn's wordscapes. It is instructive for me, adept with words as I am and conditioned to believe that whatever is written well is under control and true, to discover repeatedly that there is wisdom, including spoken wisdom, that cannot be caught in bytes on microchips. The silence of my computer keys is hardly a match for the haunting half hour's silence in heaven when the Lamb opens the seventh seal (Revelation 8:1), but just as the Apocalypse opens new vistas to the Christian imagination, so do Casey's images. And supreme among them is one that illustrates the marriage of imagination and Abbott's speculations about the territory between "this can never be" and "we know all about it."

Casey, who has spent a great deal of time with dying people, especially dying children, and who hears their messages to the rest of us with astonishing, sometimes unnerving clarity, altered permanently the way that I think about cemeteries, and hence about death, and hence about life, and hence about where we are. She said, without any fanfare, without any signal that she thought the idea remarkable, that when she visits a cemetery she thinks of herself as on the shore of the ocean of eternity, and the tombstones are the shells upon the shore.

Edwin Abbott imagined what a sphere would look like to the inhabitants of Flatland—that is, an object that could not in its totality be comprehended by them because of the peculiar limits of their particular finitude. He was anticipating Casey

Flynn's imagining how the ocean of eternity, ungraspable in its full reality by us, bound as we are in the space-time continuum, would leave traces—tombstones as seashells in cemeteries that are the shore. Like an icon that uses reverse perspective, that looks from within and thus transfigures the one who stands before it, Casey's image springs me free from limited Dimensionality and gives me a glimpse of what the grace of God might look like in its passage through my world.

ON PAYING ATTENTION

Christian answers to "When is it?" and "Where are we?" have never been easy, but they used to be easier. Time and space have always been mysterious and vast, but, when they were thought to be absolute, you could go about your life confident that things would stay put. Everything, we now know, however, is in motion—*everything.* The Letter to the Hebrews (13:8) tells us that "Jesus Christ is the same yesterday and today and forever." But what if we are no longer sure what yesterday and today and forever are? What does it mean to be "the same" in a relativistic world where simultaneity cannot, either in practice *or in principle,* be determined?

We are what we do with our attention

The late John Ciardi answered the question "What are human beings?" this way: We are what we do with our attention. We have been defined in many ways: as rational animals, featherless bipeds, the measure of all things, as forked sticks, what we eat, such stuff as dreams are made on, and a hybrid of ape and angel. The Bible says that we are made in the image of God, a little lower than the angels, that we are dust and ashes, that we fade as the flower of the field, that we are worms. "We are what we do with our attention" helps place us in the world in which we find ourselves—the world in motion. Our attention is the closest we come to having a fixed point of reference.

If "we are what we do with our attention," it would seem to follow that the more we pay attention to, the more we are. Up to a point. Mark Vonnegut, son of novelist Kurt Vonnegut, Jr., and one of my first students at Swarthmore, graduated in 1969 and published a book in 1975, *The Eden Express,* about his experience of mental illness. In the preface he says: "For a hippie, son of a counterculture hero, B.A. in religion, genetic biochemical disposition to schizophrenia, setting up a commune in the wilds of British Columbia, things tended to run together." In Mark's telling, the schizophrenia became an uncontrollable paying-attention-to-everything, the mind careening at the speed of light, avoiding sleep lest something be missed. In retrospect, he distills the horror into two sentences: "Eternal vigilance is the price of freedom. Insanity is the price of eternal vigilance."

I have not known the terror of schizophrenia as Mark has, but his artistry in *The Eden Express* has given me a glimpse of what it is like, and I know that "we are what we do with our attention" is not only an insight but also a warning. But the warning itself can be a danger. If I know the peril, I may become overly cautious, hedge my bets, stay far away from the edge of abysses, sacrifice adventure for the sake of sanity. I may lull myself to sleep chanting a jingle I once heard, "Come weal or come woe, my status is quo."

I believe that God knows that we are in this bind, and provides not an easy way out but clues for escape from the trap of playing it safe. "Revelation" is a crucial theological concept. Countless thinkers have pondered whether revelation is possible, how we would recognize it if it were, what distinguishes true revelation from false, and whether language, ambiguous and malleable, could possibly be a fit vehicle for even a true revelation. My experience of revelation neither answers these questions nor dismisses them. It does, however, shift the focus from the content of revelation to its process or method. Revelation, as I know it, is what happens when God tries to get our attention and we, reluctantly or enthusiastically or even inadvertently, give it.

"Calling attention/Isn't the same thing as explaining." These lines of the poet John Ashbery have done more than volumes of theology to illuminate revelation for me. We want explanations. We expect revelation to explain, solve our puzzles, provide assurance in the face of doubt. But when God calls attention, explanation is seldom what we get. What is offered instead is conversation and challenge.

He looked

M oses was keeping the flock of his father-in-law Jethro"
(Exodus 3:1), as he had done every day for years. Then
suddenly this ordinary day becomes one of the most momentous ever, and Moses' work is transformed. At breakfast time,
Moses is responsible for protecting sheep from wolves. By dinner time he is responsible for freeing a people from slavery.

What happened between breakfast and dinner? "He
looked" (3:2). The Bible locates a turning point of history in
the turning of Moses' head. Moses looks. What does he do
next? He pays attention to what he sees: "I must turn aside and
look at this great sight, and see why the bush in not burned
up" (3:3). Jewish legend, as reported by Louis Ginzberg, says
that God has to do something extraordinary to get Moses' attention not because Moses is a slacker but, on the contrary, because Moses is so attentive to his duty as a shepherd: Moses
"was not inclined to permit any interruption of the work
under his charge. Therefore God startled him with the wonderful phenomenon of the burning thorn-bush. That brought
Moses to a stop, and then God spoke with him."

Once Moses pays attention, his single-mindedness is itself
transformed into an instrument of divine justice. Only someone "not inclined to permit any interruption of the work
under his charge" could lead a recalcitrant people through
forty years of wandering in the wilderness. Moses becomes
Moses, becomes who he is and will be, at the moment when
he says, "I must turn aside and look." God takes the initiative:

Moses' attention is something God needs to get. But Moses' attention is Moses' to give. It was only "when the Lord saw that he had turned aside to see" that "God called to him out of the bush" (3:4).

And what does God say? I know of no better illustration of Ashbery's distinction between calling attention and explaining. God does not give Moses an explanation but calls him to attention: "Moses, Moses!" Moses acknowledges God's call— "Here I am"—and then what does he hear? No explanation now, either. "Come no closer! Remove the sandals from your feet." And then God suddenly reminds Moses of a past Moses has conveniently forgotten: "I am the God of your father, the God of Abraham, the God of Isaac, and the God of Jacob." Why has Moses forgotten this past? Because he has been brought up as an Egyptian prince in the household of the Pharaoh. Had God begun with an explanation—the Hebrews are enslaved, I have a covenant with them, you are one of them, I charge you to lead them out of bondage—Moses could have argued with God for a generation, analyzing and evaluating and thus remaining in control. It would have been the archetype of all seminars. In the meantime, the suffering would have continued and even worsened. No, God does not begin with explanation but with a call to attention. And Moses gets the point, fast: "Moses hid his face, for he was afraid to look at God" (3:4–6).

Jewish legend addresses a question that anyone might ask but that the Bible does not answer: What sort of voice does Moses hear? Our assumption that God must speak in a solemn, measured bass is reinforced by the resonant voice—his own—

that Cecil B. DeMille chose for the burning bush scene in the movie *The Ten Commandments.* Jewish legend, much cannier, knows that God would sound more like George Burns in the *Oh God!* movies. The legend says that God, so as neither to alarm Moses with loud tones nor to invite contempt of prophecy with subdued tones, addresses Moses in his father's voice. A strange and haunting suggestion, for Moses had been separated from his father just a few months after his birth. The voice would be a counterpoint of the strange and the profoundly, anciently familiar. God begins to catch Moses in a net of connections across generations, across classes, across peoples, across the periods of Moses' own life. Once you start paying attention, you begin to know webs, patterns, linkages—a knowledge from which there is no turning back except by a willful act of forgetting, a conscious change of who you are. For, as Ciardi has alerted us, we *are* what we do with our attention.

The Encyclopedia of the Dead

The late Yugoslav author Danilo Kiš, in a story called "The Encyclopedia of the Dead (A Whole Life)," evokes precisely this inexhaustible connectedness of everything. In this story, a Yugoslav woman whose father has recently died describes spending time in Sweden as a guest of the Institute for Theatre Research. "I thought," she says, "as people in adversity are wont to think, that a change of scene would help me escape the pain, as if we did not bear our grief *within* ourselves." But we learn this rationale for her trip only after she has introduced us to a truly extraordinary experience.

Being admitted alone, late at night, to the Royal Library in Stockholm, she discovers a series of dark and dusty rooms, each of which contains many volumes identified with the same letter of the alphabet. She runs to the room marked "M" (her father's initial). "I had realized—perhaps I had read about it somewhere—that this was the celebrated Encyclopedia of the Dead." The clues are plentiful, though the first time I read the story they slipped right past me: The woman is recounting a dream sequence. But her dream is so vividly portrayed, and with such a compelling inner logic, that even when the genre becomes recognizable, the line between reality and dream remains fuzzy and fluid—as is so often the case in life.

She had pictured the Encyclopedia of the Dead as "one of those esoteric creations of the human spirit that only hermits, rabbis, and monks can enjoy." But it turns out to be quite different. "What makes the Encyclopedia unique (apart from its being the only existing copy) is the way it depicts human relationships, encounters, landscapes—the multitude of details that make up a human life." By a kind of verbal and imagistic magic, the book "records everything. Everything." The compilers of the Encyclopedia are driven not by an obsessive, even schizophrenic compulsion to be complete, but by their knowledge that the smallest detail of a person's life is tied by a thousand threads of meaning and influence to everything else in the world.

The entry for her father is only a few pages long, but all the details of his boyhood home, including hawthorn bushes, the chiming of village church bells, cows mooing in their barns, the reflection of the morning sun on the cottage windows— all this is rendered as if "in a Brueghel landscape." In this single deft reference to the sixteenth-century Flemish painter whose gift for the portrayal of the intimate details of God's creation is unsurpassed, Kiš hints at the point of the story. What follows is a dazzling, even mesmerizing, profusion of details, networks, webs that gives a lively sense of what omniscience would mean, of what it means for us that God pays attention to everything. Kiš's story carries out to infinity the ripples of Jesus' remark that not a sparrow falls without God's knowing it and caring about it. And the story underlines Paul's insistence that God shows no partiality, is not impressed by celebrity. Anyone who in his or her time on earth achieved sufficient distinction to make it into one of the standard, prestigious biographical dictionaries is excluded from The Encyclopedia of the Dead, which is a kind of *Who Was, But Wasn't Who*. The compilers aim at "redressing human injustices and granting all God's creatures an equal place in eternity."

The Encyclopedia portrays the world in an infinite variety of colors: "After all—and this is what I consider the compilers' central message—nothing in the history of mankind is ever repeated, things that at first glance seem the same are scarcely even similar; each individual is a star unto himself, everything happens always and never, all things repeat themselves ad infinitum yet are unique." And God remembers it all, lest we forget.

If Danilo Kiš portrays God's paying attention, Milan Kundera, in *The Book of Laughter and Forgetting,* highlights our fickle memory, our forgetting that is part willful and part inability to take it all in and hold onto it. Kundera illustrates our capacity to avert our attention and simply obliterate vast stretches of reality, especially those parts we would rather not come to terms with, whether in the most intimate relationships—the protagonist of one of the stories tries to retrieve some old love letters in order to throw them in the trash—or in the most public events: "The bloody massacre in Bangladesh quickly covered over the memory of the Russian invasion of Czechoslovakia, the assassination of Allende drowned out the groans of Bangladesh, the war in the Sinai Desert made people forget Allende, the Cambodian massacre made people forget Sinai, and so on and so forth until ultimately everyone lets everything be forgotten."

Mission impossible

When we left Moses, he had just hidden his face, not only because of the primordial fear that to look directly at the divine would prove fatal but also out of shame, because he knew, instantaneously, that he was now linked once again to the tradition of Abraham, Isaac, and Jacob, a tradition with its attendant responsibility that he had almost succeeded in putting entirely and forever out of his mind. Those three names are all it takes to set off in Moses a speed-of-light chain reaction of remembering, connecting, paying attention to a past that was both promise and rebuke. It's as if Moses, a case study of Kundera's observation that "everyone lets everything be forgotten," has just stumbled upon The Encyclopedia of the Dead. God has interrupted Moses, has shown him a picture of the past with its characters and character restored, and Moses knows, in the twinkling of an eye, that things will never be the same again. He has responded "Here I am" to God's call, and God has put Moses on the spot by reminding him that he is not an island, entire unto himself.

Now that Moses is paying attention, God begins the explanation. (Explanation isn't a bad thing; it's all a matter of timing—it comes *after* attention is paid.) "I have observed the misery of my people . . . I have heard their cry . . . I know their sufferings . . . I have come down to deliver them." Moses perhaps breathes a sigh of relief—God has taken over; we can sit back and wait for the exodus to begin. But it is not going to be that easy. "Come, I will send you to Pharaoh to bring my people, the Israelites, out of Egypt" (Exodus 3:7–10). Moses' reply shows that he is really listening. He does not say, "But wait, God, you just said *you* have come down to deliver and bring up." Had he responded in those terms, Moses would have demonstrated that he heard the words but had not listened to what God was saying.

Moses knows that God has just given him a "mission impossible." Moses' answer to God is quite comical: "Who am I that I should go to Pharaoh?" (3:11). Anyone who has paid attention to the story realizes immediately how lame Moses' excuse is. Who is he that he should go to Pharaoh? Nephew, by adoption, of the new Pharaoh, no less. But God does not chide Moses with, "Silly man, you are his relative!" Rather, God gives Moses the most unnerving reassurance that anyone has ever received, a promise that is a challenge and is in no way an answer to the question Moses has asked.

There are regions of territory staked out by this story that still need exploring before we get to the end. I will return presently to the promise God gives Moses and ponder what it means for me. Now, though, I want to put myself in a position like that of Moses earlier in the story, when he is for the first time paying attention. Reading this story conversationally, I am not left stranded more than three millennia ago. By imagination's magic that compresses time and collapses space, I am brought right to the heart of here and now—closer to the heart than most of what I read in today's newspaper. Four moments in my life illustrate especially sharply the truth of John Ashbery's distinction between attention and explanation, four moments in which occasions and persons put it to me squarely, as God did to Moses, and said, "Listen!"

"We are tired of dialogue; we want you to listen"

In 1968, my second year on the faculty of Swarthmore College, I was asked to serve as spokesperson for the Admissions Policy Committee in an open discussion with black students, whose representatives, to express their anger at a recruitment report, had walked out of a meeting with the committee. I wrote an open letter to the campus community in which I presented the committee's case—a sort of "all deliberate speed" pledge—and said, "We do think we stand a better chance of accomplishing something worthwhile if all the black students at Swarthmore will talk to us." The all-campus meeting, attended by hundreds, took place soon after my letter was distributed. I restated, as best I could, the committee's argument and concluded with a plea that dialogue might continue.

The response stunned me: "We are tired of dialogue; we want you to listen." The committee had countless explanations for the college's lack of success in recruiting black students. Some of the explanations were based in undeniable facts. But "We want you to listen!" awakened me to see that dialogue itself can be a subtle form of domination and control exercised by those who set the agenda and fix the terminology of the discussion. As a white professor, I had a sense of entitlement to agenda-setting that seemed entirely "natural." The black students in 1968 challenged me and everybody like me, as God challenged Moses, to imagine a different world, a world of commitments that would make us uncomfortable, commitments in the face of which our familiar explanations ring hollow.

"You're being outrageous"

In 1976, biblical scholar Phyllis Trible and I were invited to lead an event called "February Meetings" at Maryville College in Tennessee, three and a half days of lectures, seminars, and informal discussion on "Who Speaks for Man?" In the opening session, Phyllis directly challenged the formulation of the question. I said that I would use the terminology but wanted the audience to understand that I intended to use the word "man" generically.

At the first of our jointly led seminars I remarked that I always began my classes at Swarthmore by saying that the requirements for the course were all listed on the syllabus, except one: "To complete the course successfully, during the semester you must say at least one absolutely outrageous thing." I wanted to jar my students loose from the caution one expressed eloquently: "Students don't like to be fooled or 'taken in.' Even if they believe something, if it seems like it could be wrong, they always cover themselves."

At the final "coffee and conversation," I asked Phyllis, who had to leave before the closing session, whether she had any parting word for me. "Yes, Patrick, for the past two days you have been absolutely outrageous." What she then went on to say prompted a conversion experience, and I spent the next day coming to terms with her challenge. What I said in the closing worship service registered the seismic shock that she had delivered to my self-satisfied system.

The depth of the shock was gauged by my choice of a biblical passage to reflect on: the very beginning of Creation, "Let there be light." I imagined how comfortable Chaos was: formless, void, and with the security blanket of darkness over its face. I wouldn't have accused Chaos of narrow-mindedness, or even of complacency. But "light" didn't speak to Chaos in a meaningful way.

I constructed a dialogue between Chaos and God. The latter keeps saying, "Let there be light." The former keeps replying, "You're just not getting through to me," just like me when I responded to "Use inclusive language" with "In my own consciousness I'm not being exclusivist when I use familiar terminology, and it's too bad if you are misled by what I say."

Phyllis had jolted me to recognize that the important thing is not what connects with my experience, or even my good intention, but the impassioned voices of millions of women who are saying that the common usage is an insult, a put-down, to them. Like Chaos speaking to God, I had been saying that women ought to be content with familiar terms. Phyllis's rebuke had made me see that when God said, "Let there be light," nothing would have happened—unless Chaos had decided to give light a try.

Three years later I sent Phyllis a copy of my just-published book, *New Directions in New Testament Study*. I thanked her for precipitating my repentance, and said that as a consequence of her reproach of my outrageous persistence in sexist language, the book didn't have a single "mankind" or "everybody . . . he" in it. I doubted that she would remember the February Meetings confrontation, since I suspected it was only one of hundreds in her experience.

Phyllis replied that she remembered the incident very well, for two reasons. First, she had never before spoken out alone on the issue of sexist language. Second, "I had," she wrote, a "fever of about 102°. After leaving Maryville, I succumbed to-tally to whatever virus it was and spent most of the following six weeks in bed. So if you heard a prophetic word, I think it must be attributed in large part to the flu. God moves in mys-terious ways."

The Maryville conversion was decisive, but it was not com-plete. Some years later I was challenged to a second-level listening. In the aftermath of Phyllis Trible's reprimand, I had advanced from inclusive language to an understanding that human relationships, including professional ones, could be non-hierarchical. From the "different voice" of women I had learned that a tapestry woven on a loom is a more humane image of our life than is the graphing of our stories along axes of success and failure.

Then, in a meeting with several female students and faculty at Swarthmore, I was stunned when a colleague, Demaris Wehr, said, "We want you for an ally, but we don't want you to tell us what to do." The remark was as startling as an un-consumed burning bush. Here I was, thinking myself a con-vinced feminist, yet still acting in the way that patriarchalists do, claiming to know what is best for others and how best to achieve it. I had learned to listen to what women were saying but had not yet learned to pay attention to what they mean when they say it.

Some years later I heard another man who was trying to break through the wall of his own sexist bias say to a woman that what was really needed was the struggle of dialogue. She replied that what was needed was his really looking her in the eye and engaging her as a human being. I realized once again how I need to be reminded, repeatedly: "I know that you be-lieve you understand what you think I said, but I am not sure you realize that what you heard is not what I meant."

A story from fifteen hundred years ago has much to teach me. Saint Scholastica, sister of Saint Benedict, tried to get her brother, when they were visiting at a house outside his mon-astery, to take seriously her request that he stay longer for further conversation with her. When he refused, she prayed, and "the very instant she ended her prayer the rain poured down. Realizing that he could not return to the abbey in this terrible storm, Benedict complained bitterly. 'God forgive you, sister!' he said. 'What have you done?' Scholastica simply answered, 'When I appealed to you, you would not listen to me. So I turned to my God, and God heard my prayer.'"

Academic resistance to women's studies, to inclusive language, to a serious recasting of syllabi and classroom dynamics in response to the feminist challenge is perfectly understandable. Feminism challenges all of us, men and women, to abandon our confidence that we know what to do, that the way we have been trained to think, argue, learn, and teach is the way to true and full humanity. Few if any of us ever thought that we were perfect, but few if any of us ever before realized how partial and deeply biased our working definition of "the human" is.

"You are <u>all</u> one"

A third occasion that got my attention took place in church. For some weeks I had been especially enjoying my work as a professor, teaching and being challenged by bright students. I would certainly have subscribed to the proposition that all people are children of God, but I subtly suspected that human worth and religious value are proportional to intelligence and that our minds are our link to God. God was the teacher, I was teacher's pet. Then, on Sunday, a seriously retarded young girl was baptized. "Know that the promises of

God are for you. By baptism God puts his sign on you to show that you belong to him." I knew in that moment, with a knowing that cut straight from head to heart, that my degrees, my languages, my books confer no status in the family of God. I had been content with Galatians 3:28: neither Jew nor Greek, slave nor free, male nor female, "for you are all one in Christ Jesus." The sacrament of baptism washed away my specially cherished prejudice, the distinction I had secretly held on to (a secret even from myself; I would never have admitted it), and I added, "neither Ph.D. nor retarded." I was devastated and liberated in the same instant.

The conversion precipitated by the baptism was reinforced in 1980 when Thomas Hoyt, Jr., a black biblical scholar I had come to know through a project at the Institute for Ecumenical and Cultural Research, and who has since become a bishop in the Christian Methodist Episcopal Church, gave the baccalaureate address at Swarthmore College.

The college's board member assigned to read the Scripture was on the verge of choosing the standard Wisdom passage from Proverbs 8:11, "Wisdom is better than jewels, and all that you may desire cannot compare with her." When she got word that the speaker wanted Psalm 139, "O Lord, you have searched me and known me," she was sure he would want her to stop with verse 18, "I come to the end—I am still with you." Verse 19, "O that you would kill the wicked, O God," with the crescendo to verse 22, "I hate them with perfect hatred; I count them my enemies," would contradict the spirit of uplift appropriate for a baccalaureate service. Hoyt insisted, as the academic procession was forming, that the final verses of the psalm were what he especially wanted the seniors and their parents to hear. She read the whole thing, but her heart wasn't in it.

The disagreement over the propriety of the reading at that baccalaureate clarified for me why I am put off when something like the Wisdom passage from Proverbs is the scriptural adornment to an academic occasion. When the Bible praises wisdom and learning, it sounds to professors as if the Word of God is giving unqualified support to academic values. The choice of Proverbs presupposes that the function of Scripture in the academy is to make professors feel good.

If one can't be simultaneously a committed academic and a committed Christian, I've done a giant con job on myself. But the function of the Bible is to challenge, not to lull. The academy needs to hear from the Bible how we are exiles, how the church was made up of not many wise, how God has chosen the foolish things of the world to put the wise to shame.

A case can, of course, be made that the Proverbs passage presents a challenge: I am not to stop short at knowledge but must move on to wisdom. But most of us who are learned suppose that we are by that fact wise—or at least we think that wisdom is waiting for us at the end of the road of knowledge, not lurking around the corner of foolishness.

"We'll scare you half to death"

The fourth occasion on which I learned to pay attention was the most personal of all. In the immediate aftermath of my father's suicide in 1983, my conflicts of feelings—anger, bafflement, shame, guilt, despair, to name a few—remained unresolved because they were unattended to. Dealing with them would have distracted me from my duties and tarnished my image of my competence and effectiveness, so precious to me and admired by others. There is, to be sure, a grace in numbness. When really bad things happen, especially when they happen out of the blue, we often get through them by shutting down for a while. When I was young, the book *God Is My Co-Pilot* provided a popular image for divine grace. The image has never appealed to me. What I thank God for is constructing me with an autopilot that kicks in when needed. In the wake of my father's death, though, I left it on far too long.

I had been warned of the well-known "anniversary problem," so I was apprehensive as May 17, 1984, drew near. When that day came and went without fazing me at all, I figured that the anniversary problem didn't apply to me. My strategy for coping had worked. Four days later, however—a year to the day after the funeral, which I had organized and orchestrated beautifully and efficiently, so that everyone present was consoled and uplifted and I was shielded from my own grief—a homicidal/suicidal fantasy of overwhelming terror signaled the grave danger into which my passion for explanation and control had thrown me.

Whether I was asleep or awake or somewhere in between, I do not know, but I was certain that I was going to walk to the kitchen, get a knife, and kill my children and then myself. I can remember to this day grasping the sides of the bed, until my knuckles ached, so that I wouldn't get up. I was sure that if my feet touched the floor, nothing—not God, not a sense of right and wrong—could stop me. When someone says about some particularly heinous crime, "I can't imagine how anybody could do that," I wince, because I can. The feelings we don't like, don't comprehend, don't know what to do with, can be ignored for a time, but they will take their revenge. It was as if the unresolved, unattended psychological issues were saying to me, "We will scare you half to death if we need to to get your attention!"

I thank God that I came to a stop and took the step that so many academics disdain on the grounds that with all our brain power and training in explanation we ought to be able to think our way out of our problems. For a long time I shared the widespread suspicion that asking for therapeutic help was weak—all right for those who needed it, but I was better and stronger than that. I now know it's a turn that takes strength. A therapist taught me, or rather helped me learn, to pay attention to a whole host of voices inside me that my entire academic training had conditioned me to filter out. To a dangerous degree I had let literature substitute for life. I marveled at the heights and depths of human experience in novels and poems and plays while scrupulously keeping my own emotions within bounds. Persuaded that the only things we can really know with our minds are those about which we care little or nothing with our hearts, I read about passionate intensity while maintaining my sweet reasonableness.

And it wasn't just literature that I thought I "understood" without really comprehending. I saw and commended in my students revolutions and revelations that I wouldn't let happen to me. I recall particularly some conversations with a Swarthmore senior, among the dozen ablest students I've ever taught, with a dazzling transcript and an imposing list of other accomplishments. She was having a rough time. Emotional realities had smashed through her intellectual defenses. Never before had she been derailed from the straight track of traditional academic achievement, never before had she asked, "Is it worth it? Is my heart really in all this? What price have I paid for what I have done?" The future no longer seemed fixed to her. I was glad that I could say in letters of recommendation for her that she admitted to not being fully prepared for all her classes that semester. Not being fully prepared was part of her preparation for life. A letter she wrote to me registered her shift into the ironic Christian mode. She spoke of her "realization that there is no unambiguous thing called 'doing good' for the world." Another student, a few years earlier, had written about "the idea that our lives have to be 'successful.' Time became a hangman's rack. If I didn't make the right decisions now and decide everything in advance, my life would be wasted."

"You're just being emotional!" is the ultimate academic put-down, often expressed with a fair degree of emotion. "Mere emotion," "merely emotional"—it is as if these words themselves constitute an argument, a Q.E.D., a magic formula that dissolves challenges so that they need not be dealt with or even faced. Yet the "mere" and "merely" are prejudicial in two senses.

First, lurking under the linguistic surface are ancient disputes about the bestial and the human, the feminine and the masculine, the civilized and the barbarian, the infantile and the mature, "Medieval" and "Enlightened," Romantic and Classic, the superstitious and the scientific, ape and angel. Emotions are relegated to the category of the primordial, a kind of chaotic stuff out of which and beyond which "we" have evolved, and the criteria for "us" are determined precisely by the negation of what we are thought to have outgrown.

Second, "mere" and "merely" suggest that the emotional is insignificant, beneath the dignity of the true scholar. Serious thinkers simply have better things to pay attention to. If I am being "merely emotional," I can hope that the aberration will soon pass, leaving little or no trace. We come to believe that the emotional is an unfortunate glitch embedded in the hardware; sophisticated software can bypass it completely. One just needs to learn the codes and implement them, exercise one's will, and get oneself together again.

I doubt that I ever subscribed fully to the equation of "emotion" with "mere emotion," but to the extent I did, it was because the emotional is scary. Indeed, "mere" is the mask we put on something that is not mere at all, but overwhelming. Maturity begins when I say either that my rationality is as mere as my emotion, or, better, that neither of them is mere at all. I am, thank God, both, and much else besides.

Responding to the Moses who is yet to be

When I read the story of Moses and the burning bush, of Moses looking and then turning aside to see, and of God speaking to him, these are the voices I hear: "We are tired of dialogue. We want you to listen." "We want you for an ally, but we don't want you to tell us what to do." "The promises of God are for everyone." "We will scare you half to death if we need to to get your attention."

At the end of the story God says, in answer to Moses' question, "Who am I that I should go to Pharaoh, and bring the Israelites out of Egypt?" "I will be with you." These would, of course, be words of the highest reassurance. What follows? "And this shall be the sign for you that it is I who sent you: when you have brought the people out of Egypt, you shall worship God on this mountain" (Exodus 3:11–12). In other words, God says, "You will know that I have been with you when you have completed the mission impossible on which I am sending you." The terms are risk, trust, and faith, as in my four moments of revelation. I learned that dialogue can nudge us, but listening can jolt us. I learned that the character of a world shaped by feminism cannot be predicted from within the world feminism radically criticizes, for explanation itself will be refashioned. I learned that since intelligence bestows no privilege in God's realm, academic prejudice is due for a complete factory overhaul. I learned that anyone embarking on a process of psychotherapy knows the plight of Moses: At the beginning there is no guarantee, only a hope that when you have done it you will know you have done it.

I have had to learn to listen to the God whose ways are not my ways, whose thoughts are not my thoughts. I am always tempted to make God over in my image, the image of the creature who forgets, whose attention either flits from here to there in a haphazard frenzy or simply crawls into a hole and falls asleep. But the ancient notion of the omniscience of God reminds me that God's responsibility, God's nature, is to know everything, like the compilers of the Encyclopedia of the Dead—not just to know everything as in a catalogue but to know everything in its intricate and inextricable connection with everything else, always and everywhere.

The Bible has no illusions about how difficult it is for God to get us to pay attention. But if the Bible shows how hard it is for us to learn to listen to what God is saying to us, the Bible also shows that God, too, practices the discipline of listening. Moses asks what appears to be a clear, direct question, "Who am I that I should go to Pharaoh?" but God replies, "I will be with you, and the guarantee is that when you have done what I am sending you to do, you will have done it." God is here responding not to the question Moses asks, not even to Moses as he currently is—"Who am I?"—but to the Moses who is yet to be, the Moses who is made in the image of God and is capable of liberating a people. God listens to what I may become, and therefore challenges me to come out of myself in order to be myself.

John Ciardi was right: We are what we do with our attention. The link between God and us who are made in the image of God is attention—the attention we pay when we look and turn aside and see, and then hear, and then act. Revelation is this whole sequence. The link can be made between breakfast and dinner, or it may take a lifetime to forge. There is no guarantee that it will happen at all. That God challenges us to use all the skills of explanation we have is for me an article of faith. That we all, repeatedly, even habitually, use our skills of explanation as a way of evading the challenge God presents to us is for me a matter of observation. That attention upsets explanation and thus deepens, broadens, and enriches life, afflicting us when we are comfortable and comforting us when we are afflicted, is for me a matter of experience.

ON HOPING AND PRAYING

Christians, if asked to account for the hope that is in them, are supposed to have something to say (1 Peter 3:15). Saint Paul missed a chance in 1 Corinthians 13, where he could have added, after "Now faith, hope, and love abide, but the greatest of these is love"—*and the toughest of these is hope.* Hope is difficult not because it is unreal or unavailable but because we think we can create and control it, and we can't. I have wasted much energy trying to figure out what gives hope or takes it away and have finally realized that these are the wrong questions. Hope is just there, it isn't something I conjure or dismiss. It is a gift of God. I suspect that it is also grounded in biology, in hundreds of millions of ancestral years of training in survival in the face of myriad threats. In other words, hope is grace and hope is nature. Both can be nurtured and hindered—but neither grace nor nature can be denied.

Negative Capability

For a long time—until I was in college, anyway—I had little sense of an "interior life." When I heard or read about the interior life of others, I was mystified. I saw this not as a challenge to explore but simply as a puzzle to understand. I believed that I could use my powers of intellectual analysis to figure out what people were talking about. I even produced an undergraduate paper arguing that poetry was what people wrote when they couldn't manage to say straightforwardly what they meant.

Breakthrough began in my junior year, thanks to one of my teachers, Paul Alpers, who shattered my rationalist illusion that poetry is frustrated prose. He gently led me through the Romantic poets to John Keats's "Ode to Autumn," where, at the end, "gathering swallows twitter in the skies," and I burst into uncontrollable tears. I was embarrassed, but there was nothing that I could do. Keats was figuring me out, not the other way round. I had understood for a long time Wordsworth's "thoughts that lie too deep for tears." Keats got through to the tears that lie too deep for thoughts. Eventually I would understand that thoughts and tears (and laughter) are tied together in the senses. Poets have ideas, of course, but so do others—professors for instance. But poets, more than professors and most other people, have to be obsessively observant, their senses on edge. They notice sounds, smells, touches. They are like one of John le Carré's spies, who "walked the wide streets, analyzing nothing, alert to everything."

The "Ode to Autumn" activated my senses and opened the gates of feeling, but the deeper reaches of spiritual life were still closed to me. What opened the way, and has continued, ever since, to serve as my compass, is the principle of "Negative Capability," enunciated by Keats in a December 1817 letter to his brothers: when one "is capable of being in uncertainties, mysteries, doubts, without any irritable reaching after fact and reason." Negative Capability, the willingness to let little brown jobs remain little brown jobs, a trait of which Keats named Shakespeare the supreme exemplar, may seem an odd beginning to an account of the hope that is in me, but resistance to certainty has proved for me a solid ground for hope.

The most serious, scariest threat to hope that I have experienced is isolation. The demonic has many faces. It has shown itself most gloatingly to me in loneliness, reinforced by a fear of abandonment that is kept alive by my father's goodbye-less death.

Letter to Alyosha

The time after my first divorce was one of excruciating loneliness. I was bingeing on Russian literature. I had read Alexander Solzhenitsyn's *The Cancer Ward,* and then turned to Dostoevsky's *The Brothers Karamazov.* I finished at midnight, and so powerfully wanted to talk about it to someone—anyone—that I drove all over Swarthmore, past homes of friends and colleagues, to see if a lit window would tell me that there was someone who might listen to me. No lights. So I returned home and wrote a letter to the youngest of the brothers.

Dear Alyosha,

It is midnight, I have just finished your story. I am alone and have no one to talk to. The few people I would care to see are surely asleep, and even the most sympathetic friend would think it extravagant to be awakened because I have been undone by The Brothers Karamazov. *The book has moved me to tears, the tears that come from deep inside.*

Why the tears? It was finally the funeral of the young boy Ilusha at the very end of the story that brought them on. That's partly because I have a little boy, and whenever something reminds me how vulnerable all of us, and especially children, are, it pierces me to the heart. Children abused, abducted, murdered: yes, Alyosha, your brother Ivan did not linger over trivial questions. "But then there are the children, and what am I to do about them?"

Ivan, the obsessive intellectual, suffers from his analysis of the world's incongruity because his thinking is laced with deep feeling. But he keeps himself apart, aloof, by contempt for those not as smart as he. The book has shaken me because I want to be like Alyosha and know that I am like Ivan. Yet I have an inkling—it's not either/or, but both/and and and and and. I continue:

The story of your unlucky family leaves the impression that we are all unutterably different from one another. Could that be because we are really all the same? It has been said of your creator, Dostoevsky, that he could find room in his soul for all the Karamazovs—you Alyosha, your impulsive brother Mitya, Ivan, your licentious father

*Fyodor, and some would add your murdering half-brother Smerd-
yakov. Is the storyteller's secret the knowledge that the human being
is a question, and though the answers are infinitely different, the
question is the same?*

*If the question is the same, then, even if it is difficult and may
be impossible to judge between answers, we can at least criticize (or
pity?) those who spend their lives answering the wrong question.
This seems to be your opinion, Alyosha. In your speech at Ilusha's
grave you imply that whatever happens to the boys individually,
they must remember that at this time and at this place they understood what the question is. Ivan said pretty much the same thing,
though in his characteristic wry way. He pointed out to you that underlying the passionate ideological disputes of your time, "it all
comes to the same, they're the same questions turned inside out."*

By this time I am fully engaged in my conversation with
Alyosha. In the letter, I introduce him to some of Solzhenitsyn's characters, whom he could not have known—they were
created a century later—but he would instantly recognize
them.

*They are in a cancer ward, where they keep discovering that their
question, which they've been taught by decades of communist ideology is entirely different from your question, is really the same question turned inside out. One of them, the one I most wish you could
meet, Oleg Kostoglotov, says, "I'm cheerful because I'm used to
suffering." A declaration worthy of a Karamazov! He replies to a
fellow-patient who has contemptuously asked, "Why read, when
we'll all be dead soon?" "That's exactly why you have to hurry,
because you'll soon be dead."*

The people in the cancer ward, directly confronted by their own stark materiality, begin to suspect that the spirit is not, as they've been taught, an opium-induced illusion floating above the material, but is, rather, what underlies everything. The condemned people in the hospital are not looking for an easy answer, and they would be suspicious if one were offered. They don't want to believe, and they don't believe much.

Why, I kept wondering while reading *The Cancer Ward,* is belief so upsetting to these people while at the same time they are clearly drawn to it? I supposed that they resisted because their ears had been tuned to too narrow a rhetorical range, and spirit-talk, soul-talk, God-talk, which is usually in the subjunctive—"maybe," "perhaps," "could be"—creates too much static. I suspected that they were attracted because their creator, Solzhenitsyn, knew that the old Russian breadth, the boundless hospitality of soul so brilliantly exemplified by Alyosha's mentor, Father Zossima, could never be squeezed completely out.

Avieta Rusanov, the bright and self-confident daughter of one of the patients who is himself insufferable in his haughty disdain for the common people he claims to revere, couldn't stand the subjunctive. She "always found it distressing when people's thoughts did not separate into clearly true and clearly wrong conclusions, but tangled and grew raveled and divided into unexpected nuances that only lent confusion to ideas."

A close brush with death momentarily softens up Avieta's father, but by the time he leaves the hospital he is as callous as ever. He doesn't even learn from his own sufferings. I suspect that people who don't learn anything are truly lost. Pavel Nikolayevich Rusanov "had no respect for people who went down in life and not up." And he remained so sure that he knew which direction is which. But does anybody, really?

I then introduce Alyosha to some of the women in the cancer ward, mostly doctors and nurses. Doctor Lyudmila Afanasyevna Dontsova, who faces many times a day the enigma that "one who takes any action brings about both good and evil," has to go suddenly to Moscow for an operation. She has detected cancer in herself. Her examining physician tells her that suffering an illness in one's own specialty is "the surest test of a doctor." And as she is thrown into a maelstrom of change, she muses, "So attached are we to the soil, yet so totally at the mercy of the winds!"

Doctor Vera Kornilyevna Gangart is one of those people for whom sensitivity is a blessing with a curse at its core. For her to establish a close relationship with anyone, "it takes scores, even hundreds of similarities and coincidental circumstances. Each additional coincidence brings them only a fraction closer, but one element of discord can pull them apart at once." She knows the acute loneliness of having "no one of whom she can ask: What am I to do? How can I live?" Isn't it just the fractions closer that matter?

I told Alyosha about what happened in his country since his time—how Lenin and Stalin and their successors had created a

frightful tyranny that obliterated the fractions in the name of a
Purpose larger and grander than the individual human life.

*Yet in face of the terror there are still people, like Solzhenitsyn, who
insist that "history moves too slowly for our lives, for our hearts."
He is right when he says, "It is not the standard of living that
makes us happy, it is the way we feel, the way we look at life." But
wouldn't you agree that he is too optimistic when he goes on to say,
"Both of these are always within our power, and hence man is always happy if he wants to be, and no one can stop him"? Yes, no
one outside me can stop me, but my own inner confusion can.*

*Father Zossima said something to you, Alyosha, that could
have thrown you off balance. "You are working for the whole, you
are acting for the future." But he did not stop there, and he showed
that he knew the fractions matter: "Seek no reward, for great is
your reward on this earth: the spiritual joy which is only vouchsafed
to the righteous man." And Dostoevsky knew that righteousness is
not always sensible. "In some cases it is really more creditable to be
carried away by an emotion, however unreasonable, which springs
from a great love, than to be unmoved. And this is even truer in
youth, for a young man who is always sensible is to be suspected
and is of little worth."*

A young person who is always sensible—Dostoevsky in a
single phrase has found me out. What I had so long thought
was my virtue turns out to be cause for suspicion.

*When Oleg Kostoglotov left the cancer ward, cured temporarily at
the price of impotence, he wandered about the town as if he were
present at the first day of Creation. He didn't kiss the earth, but he*

did go in search of a flowering apricot tree—and found one—and he also discovered that you don't get Creation without the Fall, and the Fall isn't something big and stupendous but is a lot of annoyances and unprovoked meanness. Kostoglotov is not always sensible; he even talks enigmatically of maybe being a fragment of the World Spirit. I prefer the way old Doctor Oreshchenkov thinks of it, about the meaning of existence being in the degree to which we are "able to keep unmuddied, unfrozen and undistorted the image of eternity that sits within each person. Like a silver moon in a calm pond."

The fundamental problem of Russian literature, even in my own time, is the Christological problem: how spirit and matter can coexist, how suffering can be a clue to the divine, how God and humanity can be one. You inhabitants of Skotoprigonyevsk were forced by your preoccupation with the spirit to recognize the humanity of Christ. The patients in the cancer ward, preoccupied with humanity, have begun to sense his divinity. The Christological problem is a birthmark on Russian literature, and not even the most radical surgery has been able to efface it.

Pray for Doctor Dontsova. Pray for me, Alyosha, that I be not always sensible, as I will pray for you, and as Father Zossima does for us all.

Yours faithfully,

Somebody might easily have thought that I was crazy, writing a letter in the dark hours of the morning to someone who does not exist. But on that day more than a quarter-century ago, Alyosha Karamazov was a vital participant in the communion of saints, which is for me the community that sustains hope. There are plenty of people alive today who are part of that community, but so are there many among the dead. Not only do I pray for the dead—in the letter I even ask Alyosha to pray for me and for one of Solzhenitsyn's imaginary characters.

I doubt that I realized it at the time, but writing the letter to Alyosha expressed hope and reinforced it. I came unstuck from my loneliness by not staying stuck in the everyday world. I broke free from limited Dimensionality. On that dark morning the walls between the real and the imaginary, the living and the dead, then and now, here and there, came tumbling down.

What I found in Dostoevsky's world and Solzhenitsyn's was not escape but liberation. In life, as in mathematics, to use again Albert Marden's observation, "a dimension is a degree of freedom." *The Brothers Karamazov* and *The Cancer Ward* brought to vivid life Keats's Negative Capability and Fitzgerald's juggling act as foundations for hope. The line between "my experience" and Alyosha's, Ivan's, Pavel Rusanov's, and Doctor Gangart's blurred for me almost beyond recognition. I don't need to be always sensible; I can acknowledge both the Ivan and the Alyosha in me; I needn't recoil when thoughts tangle and unravel and divide into unexpected nuances.

The tears through which I wrote the letter to Alyosha were the dividend on the tears I had deposited a decade earlier at the end of Keats's "Ode to Autumn." Then I had *understood* that the world of literature was not "out there," but could be a room of my own. Now I *knew* it. When I was writing the letter I could not have told you for sure whether I was in Swarthmore or Skotoprigonyevsk. Saint Teresa is right again: "It is extraordinary what a difference there is between understanding a thing and knowing it by experience."

We hope and pray

Hope can be nurtured in imagined worlds, but it must be exercised in the everyday world, and not just that of my immediate surroundings, but in places I hear about. On the last day of 1972, I was startled to see in print an expression that I had probably used often. A newspaper article, headlined "Sen. Scott Prays for Peace During Halt in Bombings," included this quotation from the Pennsylvania Republican and Senate minority leader: "I hope and pray that the resumed negotiations . . . will lead finally to a lasting peace [in Vietnam]." For the first time I wondered: Does the "and pray" add anything at all to the "hope"? When I hope and pray for an end to the war, do I really think that my praying adds anything to my hoping, and beyond that, do I really think that either of them does any good at all?

I noted earlier that hope, if not the greatest of the trio that includes faith and love, is probably the toughest, and has certainly been the least attended to in the history of Christian thought. One reason that we have a livelier sense of faith and love than of hope is that we know pretty well what the effects of faith and love are.

Faith expresses itself in trust and belief. Job's refusal to curse God is a concrete expression of faith without limit, and though I doubt that I would hold out as long as Job did, his story gives me a clear picture of what faith entails. We also know that faith expresses itself in creeds and dogmas and the courage of conscience: "The Word became flesh and dwelt among us"; "We believe in the resurrection of the body"; "Here I stand; I can do no other; God help me!" Faith is not easy, but because we know how it expresses itself, we at least have a notion of what we're talking about.

Love expresses itself in deeds. Sell all that you have and give to the poor; Do good to those who persecute you; Stop to help the person lying beside the road; Love one another so that everyone will know that you are my disciples; Christ emptied himself and took the form of a servant. We are unprofitable servants, but we know what it is that we are falling short of. Love is not easy, but because we know how it expresses itself, we at least have a notion of what we're talking about.

The effect of hope

But what about hope? What is its effect? How does it express itself? For many cultured despisers of Christianity, hope appears to be anti-human, the expectation of pie in the sky when we die, so that the everyday world with its human constituents and its intractable problems dwindles into insignificance.

But hope is not blind or insensitive. There is nothing authentically Christian about Pollyanna. "We hope and pray that . . ." is the clue to the effect that belongs to hope: The expression of hope is prayer. We have faith and trust; we love and act; we hope and pray. Trust is not something added to faith, action is not something added to love, prayer is not something added to hope: yet in each of these statements we are not simply repeating ourselves. We are recognizing how words become flesh.

If prayer is the proper expression of hope, we can gauge the dimensions and contours of hope by getting clear about what prayer is. Forty years ago George Buttrick, who was my teacher, pastor, and friend during my college years at Harvard, pointed out that prayer is traditionally parceled out into four categories, easily remembered by the acronym ACTS: Adoration, Confession, Thanksgiving, Supplication. The scheme probably seemed a little too neat, even artificial, at the time, but I have come to realize that the four categories taken together characterize the complex set of attitudes that makes Christian hope a virtuous and not a vicious thing.

Adoration does not come particularly easy. We are too sophisticated or too jaded to see what Isaiah saw: the Lord high and lifted up, train filling the temple, and seraphim standing around chanting "Holy, Holy, Holy." Since Jesus has taught us to call God, familiarly, "Our Father," we assume we are beyond the precautions of an Ezekiel who set up a series of verbal buffers between himself and God to shield himself from the terror of the divine majesty: "such was the *appearance* of the *likeness* of the *glory* of the Lord." Wondering and marveling seem in slightly bad taste, and one reason our hope is thin is that we find adoration embarrassing.

We are good at confession—perhaps too good at it. With the greatest of ease we confess the manifold sins and wickednesses we have from time to time committed against God's divine majesty. We admit we are not worthy that Jesus should come under our roof, but we know that he will anyway. We talk about our "shortcomings," as if it is only a matter of trying a little harder.

I had heard hundreds of times the bidding prayer: "Almighty God, to whom all hearts are open, all desires known, and from whom no secrets are hid," and had paid little attention. Then one day I suddenly understood how devastating those words are. "All hearts are open" is no real threat, since I think that I have some control over what is in my heart; "all desires known" strips away defenses, since some of my desires I would prefer to keep to myself. But then comes: "from whom no secrets are hid." This does not mean simply that I have no secrets from God; secrets from God have already been covered in "all desires known." The prayer acknowledges that God knows even those secrets I hide *from myself.* Such secrets, of course, need not all be bad. When I feel most miserable, most despairing, God knows secrets of my worth and strength that are inaccessible to me, just as when I feel most proud, most confident, God knows secrets of my treachery—secrets I not only do not admit but also am not even aware of. Original amnesia is on a par with original sin, and our confession is thin because we are uncomfortable when someone knows us more intimately than we know ourselves.

If we are not very good at adoration and confession, chances are we will not be very good at thanksgiving either. We may not be as self-assured as the Pharisee who thanked God that he was not as other people, but our thanksgiving frequently amounts to a self-satisfying enumeration of those things that make us "more fortunate" than those who are "less fortunate than we." We say we do not deserve all God's goodness to us, but in our hearts we believe, if not that we have earned it all, at least that God helps those who help themselves. I do not like being obligated to anyone, even God, and really to give thanks is to admit that there is an imbalance of payments. One reason our hope is thin is that our thanksgiving does not take us out of ourselves but makes us even more self-conscious.

Although my adoration, confession, and thanksgiving are weak, I at least know what I am doing when doing them, and why. I adore God because that is what God as God deserves, I confess what I have done, I give thanks for what I have received. With supplication, however, the fourth of Buttrick's categories, we are in a more problematic realm: the future. If I ask God to heal the sick, give peace in our time, or unify the church, I am trying to influence what is yet to happen. Maybe God sees past, present, and future as an eternal present: According to Einstein's special relativity, as I learn in *The Physics of Star Trek,* if I were traveling at the speed of light, "the entire history of the universe would pass by in a single instant." But I do not, and I wonder whether anything I do, especially praying, makes any difference at all.

Maybe our deepest longing, as Milan Kundera says, is to refashion the past, or, as one of the Jets whispers to another after the switch-blade tragedy in *West Side Story,* "Why can't it be yesterday?" How I wish the ending of the first *Superman* movie were true. Superman orbits the earth backwards so fast that time and the earth's spin are reversed past the earthquake: Dams uncrumble, cars are unburied, Lois Lane becomes undead. How poignantly I know the longing in Kurt Vonnegut's *Slaughterhouse-Five,* where Billy Pilgrim, coming "slightly unstuck in time" shortly before being abducted (as he knows he will be) to the planet Tralfamadore, watches the late movie on television, about American bombers in World War II, and sees it backwards so that the bombs are sucked up into the planes.

I do not know whether prayer makes any difference. There is no way of knowing whether my prayers for someone who is sick do any good, for example, though recent scientific research has demonstrated a statistically significant correlation between organized prayer on behalf of patients and their healing. The question of how the effect is caused remains an open one, and it is always possible to say that the improvement would have happened anyhow; or if a person who is prayed for does not get well, it is always possible to say that the suffering might have been worse without prayer. There have been billions of prayers for Christian unity, and Christians are still divided. The twentieth century has been arguably the most violent hundred years in the human story. Have the prayers for peace been too few, too lukewarm, or does praying just not do any good? We are not sure. We cannot be sure. To devote myself wholeheartedly to something about which I necessarily remain unsure, about which I cannot finally resolve my nagging reservations, to linger in "uncertainties, mysteries, doubts, without any irritable reaching after fact and reason," can seem foolhardy, and one reason our hope is thin is that our supplication is corroded by our sense of guilt about our uncertainty.

If authentic prayer is the action proper to hope, it is clear

that Christian hope is no easy, naive refusal to look reality in
the face, no escape into a fantasy land. Faith is hard, love is
hard, hope is very hard, and we can never sit back contentedly
as if they were assured possessions. Prayer may now and then
come spontaneously, but mostly it is not something we automatically know how to do. The Disciples of Christ tradition
in which I grew up trusts more than many churches the
human naturalness of prayer. Each Sunday two lay persons
offer prayers at the communion table. Sometimes my regard
for elegance of language was severely tested by this custom,
and I heard echoes of dozens of classical heresies in the words
of the well-meaning but not theologically refined elders. I
don't subscribe to the "sincerity is all that matters" excuse for
laziness or ignorance, but these people were not lazy or ignorant. Without the luxury of time and place to polish speech,
they were willing, on behalf of the congregation, to go public
with their relationship to God. Many of them labored over
those prayers. They knew that hope isn't easy. Because for
years I saw lay persons every week pray in front of others, I
find it odd that ministers and priests, the religious profession-
als, are nearly always the ones asked to pray in mixed company.
Maybe they can say it better, but there is no reason to suppose
that they have more to say.

A friend of mine says that when the disciples asked Jesus,
"Lord, teach us to pray," they were setting the agenda for the
New Testament at least as much as Jesus was when he asked
them, "Who do you say that I am?" Learning how to pray is
learning who God is. And prayer is something we have to
learn—or perhaps relearn. Robert Coles's study of the spiri-

tual life of children suggests that there is a spontaneity, a naturalness of prayer that gets buried beneath layers of distraction
and self-regard as the years pass. Another friend once told me
that her whole spiritual journey has been an effort to recover
what she knew of God as a child, knowledge that the adults in
her life kept telling her couldn't be so.

Learning to pray is high on the Christian agenda, but the
teaching is often done badly, and no church has a corner on
doing it well. Some consider prescribed prayers to be insin-
cere, while others think that spontaneous prayers are ego trips.
Prejudices about prayer run deep, and the churches have more
to learn from each other about prayer than about doctrine.

Despite its failings, we depend on the Christian community,
of which we and the apostles and martyrs and popes and bishops and monks and nuns and reformers and saints and sinners
and Sunday school teachers are all a part, to teach us to pray,
and we in turn teach others. Something that is learned can become habit, and habit can become what we call, appropriately,
"second nature." (At least once in my life the habit was nearly
lethal. I was driving three Benedictine sisters back home from
a conference. At five o'clock they said that it was time to pray.
As they began "Our Father . . ." I joined in. Conditioned by
decades of Protestant piety, I dutifully bowed my head and
closed my eyes—behind the wheel at sixty miles an hour
across southwestern Minnesota.)

The masquerade of hope and despair

But of course there is irony lurking even in the community of prayer. Hope and despair can trick us, each appearing to be the other.

How, you might ask, can despair masquerade as hope?

Earlier I referred briefly to my quoting Romans 8:28 ("We know that in everything God works for good") to a girlfriend who had just told me of her brother's early death from leukemia. Theologically ever at the ready, I quoted Paul's words to console her, and our relationship abruptly ended. What I intended as consolation had the effect of theological bludgeoning. It took a while for me to get over and through my puzzlement at her reaction, but finally I knew: The truth of a theological statement often depends on who is saying it.

I use the qualifier "often" because this is not a universal principle. If it were, my conviction about God's irony would be undermined. Of course someone who has no "right" to speak the truth can do so, as when the high priest Caiaphas, in John's Gospel (18:14), is the one who says it is "expedient that one man should die for the people." Caiaphas means one thing—that Jesus' death will pacify the crowd—but for John and his readers, Caiaphas's words mean something else entirely—that Jesus' death will atone for the sins of the whole world. In God's topsy-turvy world the blind see, the lame leap, the deaf hear, the dumb speak, liars are true, and the trustworthy lie ("I do not know the man," said Peter, and immediately the cock crowed—Matthew 26:74). Theological truth does not in principle depend on who says it.

But in practice it often does. When I quoted Romans 8:28, I was attempting to short-circuit my friend's grief. I was claiming to understand better than she did why bad things happen to good people. I was offering an easy answer to the question that would start haunting me, and never stop, when I encountered Ivan Karamazov's bottom-line challenge: What about the suffering of the children? Had my friend herself proposed Romans 8:28 as a commentary on her brother's illness and early death, the passage would have been true (unless, of course, she was using it to mask unresolved grief). She would have earned the right to speak.

This does not mean that we have to earn the consolation that comes from God's word in Scripture. No one could count the hearts ripped apart by grief that have been reknit by a reading of the Bible. Romans 8:28 is one of the great healing prescriptions of all time. But God has put us in community not so that we can quote Scripture at each other, but so that we can be present to each other. Instead of "God meant it for good," I should have said, simply, "I am here with you, and I am terribly sorry to hear about your brother." I had no business imposing meaning on her grief. Our responsibility as Christians, as human beings, is to create for each other a place in which the consolation of God's word can be received when we are ready for it.

How, you might ask, can hope masquerade as despair?

I learned the flip side of the lesson of my abbreviated college-era romance when, twenty-five years later, I flew to

Texas because my father, six years into retirement from a forty-one-year ministry in the same congregation, had closed the garage door, turned on the engine, and asphyxiated himself. When I walked into my parents' house many family friends were there. Dr. James Bledsoe, our dentist, came up to me, put his arm around me, and said, not "God meant this for good," which would have distanced him from me and been despair masquerading as hope, but "It's a son-of-a-bitch, isn't it?"—words which implied meaninglessness but brought us together, hope masquerading as despair.

Prior to that moment I would have hesitated to classify those words as a prayer, though I was half expecting, even half hoping, to hear them. Years before, I had heard the story of how, when the Bledsoes' teenage son died in a skiing accident, my father went immediately to their house, put his arm around Jim's shoulder, and said, "It's a son-of-a-bitch, isn't it?" The day my father died, when access to his meaning for me was blocked by my bafflement at his desperate act, Jim Bledsoe, by completing this "prayer circle," blessed me with my father's wisdom and laid the groundwork for a place in which, eventually, grace—aided by a skillful therapist—would give me back my father.

I have not reached the point at which I can encompass my father's death in Romans 8:28. People tell me that the pain of my father's depression (which had apparently been lifelong, though hidden almost completely from me) may have been so great that it was "better" for him to die than to continue in that pain. I used to believe without qualification that people should not kill themselves. I now recognize that there are physical conditions that may justify the desire for death, but I believe my father's conviction that the demons had won, which is how his final note put it, was mistaken. It is no consolation to me to be told that in everything God works for good. I think that one reason people have told me that my father's suicide was all right, even a good thing, is their fear that they cannot love someone who has done something wrong, especially a minister who has inspired and led them for a good part of their lives.

"I have two tales to tell, and I will tell you one"

The god Prometheus, in Aeschylus's *Prometheus Bound,* speaks one of the most haunting lines in all literature: to the tormented, baffled Io, a young woman who has caught the eye of Zeus and hence the jealousy of Zeus's wife, Prometheus says, "I have two tales to tell, and I will tell you one." Time and again the story I have thought I was telling by my life—my decisions, my actions, my inactions—turns out in retrospect to have been another story altogether. I know that everything is perceived and told from a particular point of view, but when I am in the midst of my life it is hard to accept that I may be interpreting it quite wrong. My capacity for misperception makes me cautious about both unqualified hope and unqualified despair. What about the other tale I might be telling?

We must not race too quickly past the darkened sun of Good Friday to the dawn of Easter. There is no hint in the gospels that Jesus' cry of dereliction from the cross, "My God, my God, why have you forsaken me?" (Matthew 27:46; Mark 15:34) was merely a line in a play spoken for dramatic effect. The church that gave us the New Testament wanted us to know that Christ was like us in all things, sin excepted, and the fact that he momentarily despaired shows that despair itself is not sin, does not finally cause God to turn away from us, that there's a wideness in God's mercy that cannot be exhausted even when this world, with devils filled, not only threatens to undo us but actually undoes us.

What happens when we die? An unsettling question, but this way of posing it keeps it at arm's length, a subject for theological or philosophical or medical discussion. What happens when *you* die? What happens when *I* die? Surely the question cannot come closer to home than this. But it can. The Bible faces the question: What happens when God dies?

God became a human being. The doctrine of the incarnation is a relentless assault on everything that makes sense. A baby whose swaddling clothes are dirty and need changing, a man executed as a deterrent to other potential criminals: Can this really be God? It is always tempting to think that in Christ the divine nature and the human nature operated in parallel, even in sync, but independently, without ever touching. Indeed, experience itself as we know it—the chances and changes of this mortal life—has been thought by many to be precisely what distinguishes us and the world from God. To talk of God's "experience" is to talk of God ceasing to be God.

I would like the Bible to be tidier. Surely, I suspect, God would have come to terms with death. How can I bear the terror of my own death if there is even the slightest hint that God did not go gentle into that good night? The scene at Calvary is one of stark loneliness. The one who the night before had shared an intimate meal with his friends is now all alone, dying. "My God, my God, why have you forsaken me?"

When I am radically lonely, fearing that there is no remedy, then faith, hope, and love—the virtues that abide—are not simply *inaccessible;* these ultimate, sustaining realities are literally *unbearable.* I pray to God for guidance and curse God for guiding me. I imagine utopias and abandon all hope. I suspect that all love is coercion. To speak of God to someone in the despair of unrelieved loneliness may be an assault, even if unintended. It is like the well-meaning and theologically orthodox but unfeeling ramblings of Job's friends, who richly deserve his outburst (Job 16:2): "I have heard many such things; miserable comforters are you all."

The Bible tells us that God cares not out of a sense of moral obligation or from sentimental pity but because God knows. God instinctively sides with Job, not with the comforters. Imagine Peter present at Calvary. He hears Jesus cry out, "My God, my God, why have you forsaken me?" Always the intervener, always the one who knows what to do, Peter might immediately reassure Jesus: "No. God has not abandoned you. In fact, Jesus, remember that you *are* God." Peter would then surely have heard a rebuke that he had heard once before: "Get behind me, Satan!" (Matthew 16:23; Mark 8:33). Just as the prophet Hosea portrays God's excruciating knowledge of love—I cannot abandon a wayward, faithless Israel even though I would very much like to—so the evangelists portray

God's knowledge of loneliness: God knows the absence of God.

God's death is no easy passing over, no falling asleep, no pie in the sky. Jesus "breathed his last," Mark (15:37) and Luke (23:46) tell us: just the way you will breathe your last, the way I will breathe my last, the way our mothers and fathers, stepfathers and stepmothers, our spouses and ex-spouses, our partners and significant others, our brothers, sisters, daughters, sons, stepsons and stepdaughters, our friends and enemies have breathed, are breathing, or will breathe their last. The gospel is no neurotic refusal to face death. It is just the opposite—a refusal to evade it. God died. My mind boggles at the thought that God has gotten to the other side by going through despair to get there.

Truth inside

Persons in despair turn frantically to others in hopes of finding the answer, despite their own impenetrable conviction that there is no answer. The trouble is, in a sense they are right. No one else has an answer to impose on them. Truth that comes from outside bears all too easily the aspect of rebuke. The answer that is promise, and not threat, is locked away inside me, and it is an unexpected answer—the only kind, after all, that can do an end run around an unanswerable question. The answer is the discovery that the question "What happens when I die?" is not the ultimate question, as our culture has tried hard to persuade me that it is. Not even death, the gospel tells me, separates me from God, for God has died.

"Father, into your hands I commend my spirit" (Luke 23:46) is not the conclusion of a bargaining process. Jesus does not say, "I give you my spirit in exchange for the resurrection day after tomorrow." In this part of the story, Luke leaves it at "he breathed his last." The ultimate question is not "What happens when I die?" but "In whom can I trust to the end?" I am called to trust in God who sides with Job, who "will not let go of my people," who dies alone. The gospel makes the odd sort of sense that we encountered in the resolutions of Jonathan Edwards, whose trust in God lay far deeper than the question "What happens when I die?"

Death can be a challenge to hope, but so, oddly, can the delay of death. Nicolas and Militza Zernov, eminent Orthodox scholars who lived in Oxford, England, recounted to me a visit that they had in 1963 with their good friend, C. S. Lewis, in the hospital. Suffering a lingering and excruciatingly painful cancer, he had been in and out of comas. On this particular visit he told them that the period prior to the coma he had just emerged from had been the worst of all. "I really hoped that I wouldn't wake up again." But, the Zernovs went on to say, the characteristic glint came into the irrepressibly curious Lewis's eyes, and he added, "I always did wonder how Lazarus felt!"

A *New Yorker* cartoon shows a bearded, flowing-robed prophetic type carrying through the downtown streets a placard that reads, "Yesterday in this space I predicted that the world would come to an end. It did not, however. I regret any inconvenience this may have caused." To practice hope, I must deal creatively and steadily with the inconvenience caused by the stubborn fact that the world just keeps on going. I find

Paul's words in Romans 8:23–25 more reassuring than the declaration a few verses later about God working for good in everything. He says that we are waiting for adoption as children of God, and since hope that is seen is not hope, we wait for it with patience. To wait with patience is not to sit back and do nothing; quite the contrary. Indeed, Paul uses the image of labor pains, the very opposite of sitting back and doing nothing, to illustrate the activity and striving that go with the patient practice of hope. We characteristically fix on the "negative" in Keats's Negative Capability, but the key to the phrase is "capability." If I am being truly faithful, I don't require that I see, immediately, or even ever, the fruits of my labor. God instructs Moses (Deuteronomy 32:49–52) to ascend Mount Nebo, "across from Jericho, and view the land of Canaan . . . you shall die there on the mountain that you ascend. . . . Although you may view the land from a distance, you shall not enter it."

ON WHY I AM (BECAUSE YOU ARE)

I think, therefore I am." Like most products of Western culture, I have been trimmed to fit this portrayal of human nature classically formulated by René Descartes in the seventeenth century. Descartes is in eclipse these days, but the conviction that my thought makes me what I essentially am is embedded deep. Thinking comes easily to me, so the conviction is not only deep but also gratifying: if thinking makes me me, and I think well, then, to adapt a phrase of my father's good friend, baseball Hall of Famer Dizzy Dean, "I may not be the greatest, but I's up there amongst 'em." The conviction, though, despite its appeal, is a huge mistake. When I used Descartes, as elaborated by a whole intellectual and academic culture, as my guide, I got the world wrong. I have spent much of my life trying to unlearn Descartes' lesson.

Others aren't optional

A friend from Kenya, Isaiah Muita, told me, "In Africa, we say 'I am because you are.'" The simple, succinct phrase expresses something that I had suspected for a long time but had not found the words for. The African portrayal of human nature offers a version of who I am radically different from the one bequeathed by Descartes. It tells me that I cannot start from scratch, that it is not by chance, nor is it optional, that I find myself among others. I wish that I had known the African phrase sooner so that I could have offered it to a student who wrote to me, "Sometimes I think I could just sit down and figure out my mind, but it never works that way. There are too many tangents and I never know what I want or how to go there. . . . Even in a crowd I feel very much myself, as if the world were just there, and I here." The world *there,* I *here:* this is the fix that Descartes' radical doubt gets us into. Descartes concluded that the *only* thing he could be sure of was his own consciousness.

There is a nobility in Descartes' dogged refusal to go beyond what evidence he was willing to admit, but the African approach is no less reasonable than his. And even if there are times when "hell is," in the famous line from Jean-Paul Sartre's play, *No Exit,* "other people," that circle of hell is not as deep as the one where radical loneliness dwells. "I am because you are" forces me to take others into account—and links my identity, inextricably, to a larger community.

Community is a mixed blessing. If "I am because you are,"

you have a power over me, over my very identity, that I may be reluctant to delegate to you. Or I may not be reluctant enough. One of my students in a course on Religious Autobiography expressed a trembling that I can still feel nearly twenty years later: "What came to me was a revelation, and by their nature they don't have antecedents, just contexts. It suddenly occurred to me, in answer to some question, that up to this point in my life I had never thought of myself as a responsible being in the first person. I had lived always as if for someone else, somebody who might come and repossess my life at any moment. I was stunned."

This fear of repossession is the shadow side of the wealth that I gain from others' investments in me. In Acts (20:35), Luke quotes Paul quoting Jesus: "It is more blessed to give than to receive." Like many Americans, I find it more difficult to receive than to give. In the frontier spirit I do not want to be obligated to anyone. As soon as I receive something, I make a quick subconscious calculation to determine what I must do in return to even the balance of payments, or tilt it slightly in my favor. My stiffest resistance to the grace of God is my uneasiness when I get something for nothing. This rather common pang of conscience is extra sharp for preachers' kids, who love the advantages that come because church members are generous to the clergy (I especially remember free tickets to box seats at ball games) but are embarrassed when telling their friends about such good luck. When largesse becomes routine, you start to think you deserve it, and the embarrassment gives way to arrogance. Little Jack Horner, isolated from his friends, sits in a corner eating his Christmas pie, sticks in his thumb and pulls out a plum and says, "What a good boy am I!" It is hard to fashion a community out of Little Jack Horners.

At the end of my sophomore year in college a variant of "I am because you are" yanked this Little Jack Horner out of his corner and set me down in the midst of others. I was returning home by plane. A fellow student, glancing out the window, said to me, "Just look at all those people down there, knee-deep in the little messes they call their lives!" I admired this as a sophisticated, educated observation, one of those insights that we were in college to get. After landing, on the way home, I mentioned the remark to my parents, confidently expecting them to be impressed. My father fixed me with a stern eye, and said, "Yes, but they're doing the best they can with what they have." Later, marital crises taught me that all of my education and trained rational insights still left me incapable of dealing with many parts of my life. I found out that I, like "all those people down there," had to "do the best I could with what I had."

But, thank God, my resources were not restricted to what I had. "I am because you are," while periodically threatening, is in the long run hopeful. When I have been at the edge, others have stood there with me. When self-confidence crumbles, especially when it is the hugely bolstered self-confidence of a well-educated, white middle-class American male who came of age in the 1950s, the collapse can be devastating. Had I been only because I think, not because others are, the pieces might not have gotten put together again.

Learning from the monastery

I must have suspected that the individualist culture in which I was thriving was somehow not right, not good for people, because I gravitated toward the study of monasticism. Nothing in my surroundings as I was growing up pointed me in this direction. Monastic values were the stuff of cultural contempt: Marx claimed that poverty is no virtue, Freud that chastity is neurotic, and Nietzsche that obedience is a trait of slaves. I had hardly ever met a monk or nun before my mid-thirties, well after my graduate study at Yale University—which included a dissertation on a Byzantine abbot—was finished.

My interest in monasticism, wherever it came from, has persisted, and for the past fifteen years has deepened as I have worked next door to Benedictine monasteries for men and for women. A half century ago monasticism erupted as a cultural force with the astonishing success of Thomas Merton's autobiography, *The Seven Storey Mountain*. His account of his pilgrimage from the frontiers of secularism to the austere silence of a Trappist monastery in Kentucky sold half a million copies in the first six months following publication in 1948. More recently, in her books *Dakota: A Spiritual Geography* (1993) and *The Cloister Walk* (1996), Kathleen Norris has similarly touched a nerve in our culture. "I am because you are," which caught the attention of Merton's contemporaries and is catching that of Norris's, would have sounded like gibberish in the interim during which I staked my professional claim. In an ironic twist, what started out as an esoteric, conventionally academic interest in a form of life out of phase with the world around me turns out to be the latest thing.

Independence, autonomy, authenticity—whether in Freud's guarded aim of holding compulsion at bay, or in Jung's sunnier goal of individuation, or, finally, in the high noon of "I'm OK, You're OK"—are believed to be grounded in spontaneity: "Do what you want to do," and pay no heed to the voices, whether of authorities or your own, that say you ought to do otherwise. Surely, then, the monastic life is the codification, the refinement, of everything that the psychological revolution set out to overturn, for monks are supposed to do what the superior says to do, not what they feel like doing. Monastic profession appears to be the final, irrevocable rejection of the chance to become a fully realized human being.

If the life of a monk or nun were simply a tale of submissive compliance, the charge would stick. But the abbots and prioresses whom I know are quick to quash any illusions that their brothers and sisters are docile sons and daughters, and the monks and nuns whom I know are remarkable for their individuality, their dogged resistance to fitting into the same mold. For the key notion is not obedience, although this is part of their vow, but discipline. Discipline seems out of phase with spontaneity, but it is precisely here that monasticism has patiently nurtured an insight almost totally lost in our culture, namely, that discipline is the precondition for spontaneity.

Christian monks and nuns have been living parables of discipline for a millennium and a half. Their insight into discipline and its intimate, essential relation to spontaneity is captured unforgettably in a single sentence at the end of the Prologue to the Rule of Benedict, the charter for their way of life—"As we progress in this way of life and in faith, we shall run on the path of God's commandments, our hearts overflowing with the inexpressible delight of love." You would have to search long in the psychological literature to find a definition of spontaneity to match "inexpressible delight" for sheer pinpoint accuracy.

Such delight does not come easily. If you want to learn to pray spontaneously, you do not sit around waiting for prayer to come. You pray at seven in the morning and noon and seven at night whether you feel like it or not, and one day you may catch yourself praying at another time. Benedict knew what psychotherapy has helped me learn: that when I think I am acting freely I am almost always the victim of habits and compulsions that have me in their control. "I think, therefore I am" is not a declaration of independence. It is an admission that I am stuck.

The Benedictine monastery is a testimony to "I am because you are." But oddly, or maybe not so oddly, commitment to community guarantees individuality. The abbot or prioress is to pay attention to everyone's idiosyncrasies; everyone is to be listened to, especially the younger; all the members of the community are to honor one another. Somebody, finally, has to make decisions, and there is no doubt who that is, but the test of the abbot's or prioress's leadership is the quality of the listening that has preceded the decision, not the decision itself. The Rule of Benedict trusts the intelligence and the wisdom of the people to a far greater degree than does the Constitution of the United States. The abbot or prioress is to listen not because that is the way to disarm the opposition but because paying attention to others is the way to hear God speak. Benedictine listening is very different from an opinion poll; it is almost its opposite.

Saint Benedict's Monastery, not far from where I live and work, and many of whose members I know, elected a new prioress a few years ago. It was not politics as we are used to it. The process for discerning the community's needs before considering personalities was so sacrosanct that up until the very last day the mandated response to the suggestion of a particular name as a candidate was a firm but gentle, "Sister, this is not a conversation I wish to have at this time." The process was not to be short-circuited, and took many months. It has been used in other monastic communities, but never before on the scale of Saint Benedict's. To make sure that the hopes, fears, and dreams of every one of more than five hundred sisters were heard required a patience all but unimaginable in today's political and institutional life, and I suspect there were sisters who thought the whole enterprise an unaffordable luxury and waste of time. It would have been easy, and entirely plausible, to say, "This plan is a nice ideal, but we have to be practical."

Because monks and nuns know what it means to say "I am because you are," they practice discipline to become spontaneous and then respect the spontaneous individuality of their brothers and sisters. "I am because you are" works only if I am not playing a charade and not forcing you into my mold. It also works only if none of us is making a sharp distinction between the spiritual and the everyday. Anthropologists, accustomed to dividing things between sacred and secular, come to the monastery, hear about prayer and work, and easily fall into the trap of assigning prayer to the sacred and work to the secular, with an offhand tribute to monasticism for getting these two realms into some sort of balance. But that gets it all wrong, for prayer and work are not subsets of the categories "sacred" and "secular." They are clues to a whole different way of conceiving the relation between God and the world.

The chief characteristic of the monastic life is its ordinariness, a word of revelation today when spiritualities are proliferating and competing, each intent on escalating the intensity of its claims and the extravagance of its terminology. Many of the current spiritual options insist on breaking down the sacred/secular distinction, but the very stridency of their insistence belies their fixation on the dichotomy. Meanwhile, monks and nuns go quietly about the business of living a coherent life as they have been practicing for about fifty generations, grounded in Chapter 48 of the Rule which is called "The Daily Manual Labor," and which proceeds to talk about prayer and reading as well as what the title suggests. The apparent distinction between worship and work, a distinction that signals "sacred versus secular" to the unwary and inattentive, is obliterated by the monastic manner of life, which is of a piece, not sacred and secular spliced together.

Experimental, not an experiment

History is littered with memories of utopian communities. Such enterprises are often classified as "experiments," and they provide rich material for speculation on why such experiments fail. It is tempting to think of monasticism as a utopian experiment that succeeded. But monasticism is fundamentally not utopian, for the hallmark of utopian experiments is that they are not at all experimental. They presuppose a clear and precise portrayal of the human good, an ideal to which everyone is to aspire. They tend for this reason to become authoritarian, for the person in charge knows the die in which everyone is to be cast. The life of the utopian community is an experiment but is in no way experimental.

The monastery, on the other hand, is experimental but is not an experiment. The pattern was set at the beginning. The very first Christian monk, Anthony, late in the third century went into the desert not because he knew what he should be but to experiment with what he might become. The Rule of Benedict, written early in the sixth century and gathering up and filtering the vast accumulated monastic experience of the more than two hundred years since Anthony had shown the way, manages one of the neatest tricks in the history of human organization: It codifies and regulates an experimental way of life. Benedict does not try to format everyone the same way. To be sure, one of the glories of the monastery is that when the shoemaker and the king adopt the habit, their former distinctions are done away; but those distinctions were artificial in the first place. In the monastic community, the true individuality of the king and the shoemaker, their distinctness as images and likenesses of God, can come to life.

Recognizing the anti-utopian character of the monastery has helped me finally to make sense of something about the Rule that puzzled me for a long time. Why, I wondered, is so much of the Rule devoted to seemingly interminable discussions of which psalms are to be said when? When I use the Rule itself as an aid to devotion, those chapters seem dry. But now I know that the psalms are the key to the whole enterprise, for it is they, ringing all sorts of changes on human nature and its relation to the divine, that remind the monk and nun every day, several times a day, that there is no simple, uniform blueprint according to which the person of God is designed. In a single day the Benedictine rails against God, praises God, bargains with God, basks in the glories of nature, trembles before nature's terrors, thanks God for other people, and asks God to destroy them all.

Like another crew of ironists, the characters in Greek tragic drama, the Psalmists tend to exalt God when they are in trouble and become wary of God when they are too successful. To dig your spirituality out of the Psalter is to build a sturdy defense against any tendency to utopian illusion. People on the outside assume that monastics are striving to attain an ideal. Those on the inside are instantly suspicious of anyone who claims to know for sure what the ideal is. Monks and nuns are constitutionally experimental, and will not let anybody turn them into an experiment.

American women Benedictines, in the volatile period since the conclusion of the Second Vatican Council in 1965, have overcome a centuries-long effort to turn them into an experiment. Ironically, the revolution was inspired by a directive from the male hierarchy, the very authority that had regulated them in the first place. Among people I know, contemporary American Benedictine women win the gold in the Ironic Christian Olympics.

Vatican II instructed each religious order to recover the aims and spirit of its founder. The Benedictine Sisters studied the sources and discovered that their life was being lived not according to the spirit of Saint Benedict but according to the forms of eighteenth- and nineteenth-century practice as codified in the church's Code of Canon Law. What was "traditional" was itself an aberration within the tradition.

Much of the regulation of the sisters' life was designed to protect them from "the world," which was seen as a threat to contemplation and to chastity. The customs led to countless anomalies: For instance, would the school teacher, after a meeting with parents, join them in refreshments, or leave because she was not supposed to eat with secular persons? In such ways the sisters experienced inner conflicts of role-definition and hence of self-definition. But the anomalies went deeper—into the creation and maintenance of a mentality that worked against the development of a genuine community within the monastery. Just as sisters were supposed to avoid contact with outsiders, so they were to be wary of attachments to insiders: It was assumed that to love everyone, you couldn't love anyone in particular. Life was so communally organized that real community was hard to nurture: Even recreation was required of everyone in the same room at the same time. There was little opportunity for the solitude upon which true companionship depends, and for particular friendships, which are in fact a necessary basis of friendship for the whole community.

In the heady atmosphere of Vatican II's aftermath, sisters were surprised and exhilarated as they came to recognize strengths and competencies in one another and in themselves, and developed confidence to take risks. They began to suspect that obedience could be, as Saint Benedict had intended, an open door on freedom, not one shut in its face. But they could not know where all this would lead them. Revolution meant a new and unspecified kind of future, for which the sisters were giving up the satisfaction and security of the knowledge, expressed to me by a Benedictine friend, that "What I am doing now I will also be doing on the day I die."

Sisters are now in a future which they could at best have dimly foreseen in the early 1970s. Today they ask each other, half incredulously, "Did we *really* do those things back then?" yet they can still affirm that who they are now is not radically discontinuous with who they were then. But back then, their life now would have seemed a fantasy. They go out alone, visit their family homes frequently, wear ordinary clothing, send and receive uninspected mail, develop friendships with men, and have special friends within their own community. Very likely, back then they would have been repelled by a vision of their current life.

From the pre–Vatican II perspective, the way they live now would have appeared almost indistinguishable from the life that they had renounced in order to become religious in the first place. However restive an individual sister might have felt under the pre–Vatican II system, she would characteristically have interpreted her restiveness as a sign of the distance she had yet to go in her pursuit of religious perfection. It would not have occurred to her that her uneasiness might be a protest from the depths of her Benedictine commitment against the outward manifestations of that commitment.

In the years after the Council, however, when recent practice was measured against ancient tradition, many women came to the conviction that a style of life radically different from what they had been doing was in fact a more adequate expression of the principles that had originally inspired them to make lifetime vows. Before Vatican II, those principles— summed up in the promise to seek God after a monastic manner of life—were filtered through a deep suspicion of the world. After Vatican II, the way back to Saint Benedict's simplicity and moderation was cleared, and the sisters could seek, in words that form the title of a book by Joan Chittister, OSB, *Wisdom Distilled from the Daily.* Moreover, while rediscovering ancient sixth-century tradition, the Benedictine women also recovered an enlivening feature of medieval life. To me the most striking feature of Ellis Peters's *Brother Cadfael* novels is their portrayal of the blurred boundaries between monastery and village. Monks and nuns in the Middle Ages were hardly cut off from society at all. The monastery wall was a thoroughly permeable membrane, with movement across it in both directions.

Monastics have relearned what Saint Benedict knew, and have in turn taught me, that real community is a gift, not something you construct. There is nearly everywhere today an intense, even desperate, longing to experience "I am because you are," and people are devising all sorts of schemes for "building community." The monastery is a living witness to the truth that community is something that happens when the environment is right, when hospitality is grounded in discipline and discernment, when prayer and work are rightly ordered. The Rule does not construct community. It hints at the necessary conditions.

I have learned much about those conditions from the nearby monasteries. I have learned about them as well from the citizens of Lake Wobegon, Garrison Keillor's mythical town also located very near to where I live and work. (Keillor began his radio career about three hundred yards from where I sit typing these words.) A study of American culture, *Habits of the Heart,* says that "communities of memory" are essential to a civilization, and that we dangerously lack such communities. As if setting out to confirm the analysis, hardly any of the responses to the *Life* magazine query about "The Meaning of Life" reflects even indirectly an identity formed by either community or memory, much less by a community of memory. Keillor, however, answers *Life*'s question with words learned in catechism class: "To know and to serve God, of course, is why we're here."

His answer would be readily understood by the parishioners of Lake Wobegon Lutheran and Our Lady of Perpetual Responsibility. Keillor's "News from Lake Wobegon" on his weekly radio show, "A Prairie Home Companion," portrays "the little town that time forgot," but the little town has not forgotten time. The people know one another, they gather, they gossip. Keillor's love and respect for small-town life lets him poke fun without contempt. In the Chatterbox Cafe people literally pass the time—they pass the traditions of their people from one generation to the next, forming and sustaining a community of memory that clearly has a magnetic pull on the hearts of today's amnesiac Americans, including me. Catholics and Protestants in Lake Wobegon have their differences, to be sure, but more often than not they recognize how comical their feuding is, and some of the richest moments on "A Prairie Home Companion" are the times when the pastors and their congregations break through the barriers. Hospitality invites to prayer before it checks credentials, welcomes to the table before administering the entrance exam.

Ever needful of the minds of others

If "I think, therefore I am," my thinking has a clear and cogent role to play in the world, at least in *my* world. If "I am because you are," the function of my thinking is not self-evident. When I was in graduate school, like many of my peers I began to doubt that I could justify the life of scholarship in a world where there is so much intense suffering. The example of Albert Schweitzer, who at age thirty-eight, in 1913, already a world-renowned New Testament scholar, organist, and authority on Johann Sebastian Bach, had become a medical missionary to Africa (where his work won the 1952 Nobel Peace Prize), and who died at age ninety in 1965, when I was halfway through my doctoral program, was a standing rebuke to those, like me, who had not turned, and probably would not turn, from the library to the field hospital. "You're just an intellectual, out of touch with the real world, spinning theories while the world is hurting": nobody said this to me in so many words, but nobody had to—I was saying it to myself. I suspected that my mind was a millstone hung round my neck instead of a building block for the temple of God, a dimly burning wick to be snuffed out under a bushel basket instead of a lamp to be set on a lampstand to give light to the church and the world.

Is there a ministry of the thoughtful? The question has been around a long time. A second-century critic of Christianity mocked the church, which he caricatured as making this appeal: "Let no one educated, no one wise, no one sensible draw near. For those abilities are thought by us to be evils. But let anyone ignorant, anyone stupid, anyone uneducated, anyone who is a child, come boldly." The critic then continued his taunt: "By the fact that they themselves admit that these people are worthy of their God, they show that they want and are able to convince only the foolish, dishonorable and stupid, and only slaves, women, and little children." Ancient culture's prejudices are packed into this snide remark, but the Christian church, despite its own continuing bondage in many ways to precisely those prejudices, has properly refused to worship human intelligence.

The problem of the church in America today is not too high a regard for intellect. Anti-intellectualism is a deep strain in American culture. The phrases that we use to caricature scholars—*absent-minded* professors who are *lost in thought*—reveal a lot about our contempt for thoughtful inquiry. The suspicion of the mind is also reinforced by the Western split between thought and emotion. I have at times experienced my mind as alien, as the nub of the contradiction between what I know and what I feel. If faith is supposed to put me together, if truth is supposed to make me free, and I find that my mind puts me asunder, I am going to shy away from the apparent crisis in my identity as a thoughtful Christian.

Among the many memorable phrases turned by my teacher Jaroslav Pelikan, none has meant more to me than his distinction between "traditionalism: the dead faith of the living" and "tradition: the living faith of the dead." From the living faith of many early church writers, and from none more than Saint Augustine, I have learned that my problem is rooted not in a conflict between thinking and faith, but in a cramped notion of thinking. Augustine, confronting head-on our ideal of objective, dispassionate knowledge, maintains that we can truly know only what we truly love. No challenge presented to the modern world by the Christian tradition is more radical than this insistence that knowledge and love are inseparable, even at some profound level indistinguishable. For as long as I can remember, my favorite hymn has been the ancient Irish "Be thou my vision, O Lord of my heart," which presents an image of knowledge that could hardly be farther from arm's-length objectivity: a vision, a *thou* rather than an *it,* an obedient heart. Over the years of my growing up, the hymn had quietly prepared me for the revelation that Augustine brought.

The words of Muita, my Kenyan friend, "I am because you are," extricated me from the trap of "I think, therefore I am." Augustine linked head and heart. Still, there was the haunting fear that thinking, even enriched thinking, is a luxury the world cannot afford. But a twist of the tongue finally put Albert Schweitzer in perspective, so that his renunciation of the library in favor of the hospital no longer stood, in my own thinking, as an implied rebuke of my not doing likewise. One day, my (now former) mother-in-law, repeating the familiar table grace in which we ask God to "give us grateful hearts for all your mercies and make us ever mindful of the needs of others," asked God instead to make us "ever needful of the minds of others." After thinking about it for a while, I decided that what sounded like a hilarious blooper was truly inspired.

Ever needful of the minds of others—the phrase suggests the many facets of the ministry of the thoughtful. First, those of us whom God has gifted with the capacity to ponder, analyze, and speak are ever needful of those capacities in others who have them. Second, those in the church who do not have the time or the training or the inclination to engage in patient thought need what the thoughtful can offer. And third, since theology is, in its root meaning, a word about God, and every Christian has a word about God, the thoughtful need the minds of those who are not characteristically articulate, even if—especially if—that word is expressed in ways that are unfamiliar to those whose language patterns and habits make sustained discussion relatively easy.

This third facet of the ministry of the thoughtful, the one that tells me to shut up for a while and listen, became startlingly clear to me when my great-aunt Josephine Henry, a high-school graduate who worked more than forty years in the accounting department of Texaco, invited me to teach a Sunday school class of which she was a lifelong member. It was about halfway through the session. My mind was operating on two levels (the lesson, and my marveling at the way my great-aunt had for decades been faithfully visiting the needy and caring for them, without fanfare), when it suddenly struck me: If I'm lucky, and God is good to me, I, with all my languages and book learning, may some day understand half of what Aunt Josephine *knows* about the Bible. But I did not conclude that my work is worthless. Rather, when I understand the mind as the Bible understands it, so that knowledge and love, head and heart, are interwoven, I see that the ministry of the thoughtful, far from being a condescending elitism, is a clear and cogent expression of Christian community, of "I am because you are." Aunt Josephine was proud of me, and I would do her no honor by minimizing the value of what I do. The ministry of the thoughtful is only one gift among the many that God gives to the church, but it is a gift not to be treated lightly.

There are many reasons why I am needful of the minds of others. First, I can never know enough myself. In a true community of inquiry, scholars seek not to overwhelm each other with learning but to help each other deal with the overwhelming vastness of what there is to learn. Soon after arriving at Harvard I heard a story about the writer Thomas Wolfe who, as a new undergraduate, stood in front of Widener Library and vowed to read its every book. For several weeks he devoured them at a phenomenal rate but eventually abandoned his quest when he learned that the acquisitions department was logging in volumes hundreds of times faster than he was reading them. When I admit, as I must, that what I need to know far exceeds the knowledge I can ever acquire, I am tempted to finesse the problem by saying, "I know Christ, and that is all I need to know." But this can hide the fact that my understanding of Christ is mediated through the church, the community of believers which includes not only my contemporaries but also all those who through the centuries have gone before me in the faith. Time is no barrier. I read dead people and often find them alive in a way that living people aren't. Finally, if I were to claim that God gives me direct knowledge of Christ, I know that even such an understanding of how knowledge comes to me is the result of intense debate and sustained pondering by other thoughtful Christians.

If I am needful of the minds of others because alone I can never know enough, I need them also because even what I do know is distorted. For a long time I naively thought that in criminal trials the most weighty evidence would be eyewitness testimony, but then I read an analysis of such testimony that makes clear its almost limitless unreliability. I knew that my memory plays tricks on me, that it is a hall of mirrors, but it was a shock to learn that our perceptions, constituting our immediate experience of events, are themselves deeply colored by our hopes and fears, by the vocabularies we have inherited and the emotions we have nurtured.

There is of course nothing new about this recognition of the partiality of our knowing. The monk Dorotheos of Gaza perceived the unreliability of eyewitness testimony in the sixth century. He tells of three men passing another man on the street. The first thinks the man is looking for a prostitute. The second suspects the man is a thief. And the third imagines he is on his way to meet a friend to pray. "All three men saw the same man, in the same place and, similarly, each one thought his own thoughts about him, each one according to his own state of mind." While there is nothing new about the knowledge that our knowledge is distorted, admission of this uncomfortable truth is as new as today's science. A seismologist, commenting on a feature of some geological formations in the Southwest that had been misinterpreted for decades, said straightforwardly, "Sometimes people just don't see what they don't expect to find." I cannot deny the close parallel to the way in which I close myself off to the truth of other people when I jump to the conclusion that "he is just a liberal" or "she is just a conservative."

I cannot know enough. What I do know is flawed. These two features of the *content* of my knowing would by themselves be more than sufficient reason for me to ask God to keep me ever mindful that I need the minds of others. But there are even deeper reasons, rooted in the very *ways* in which I know. We know different things; more important, we do our thinking and knowing differently.

What about the acrobats?

W hy, when praying for others, do we never mention the acrobats?" Ever since a student asked me this question, I have tried faithfully to remember the acrobats in my private devotions, and have occasionally included them in public prayers. The student's concern not only reminded me of whole realms of human experience that I tend to overlook but also pointed to experiences that fashion whole different views of the world. Lawyers, industrial workers, flight attendants, acrobats, doctors, taxi drivers, people standing in unemployment lines, legislators, piano teachers, social workers, corporate vice presidents, bartenders, radio announcers, the homeless, opera chorus singers, farmers, junior high school principals, checkout clerks—all have their special ways of knowing. One of the very few absolutely true things I've ever learned was taught to me one college summer vacation when I was working on a construction project in Dallas. The temperature was 110° in the shade, and I wasn't in the shade. I was carrying some concrete blocks. A seasoned laborer approached me with a wheelbarrow, gently but decisively took the blocks from me, and said, "Patrick, it's always better to roll than to tote." He *knew*, and knew well, in a way that I didn't.

It is a misfortune for the church that one kind of knowing—that of professors—has become the norm for Christian knowledge. Academic knowing is an honorable kind of knowing, but it is only one kind. People in the churches resent the efforts of academics to drown them out, and in the process everybody loses. Academics become defensive, maybe even contemptuous, and others become suspicious of the mind.

But there are distinctions in ways of knowing that are even more profound than those based in life experience. The Roman Catholic and the Protestant, despite all their differences, are more like each other in their ways of knowing than either is like the Eastern Orthodox Christian. As I have already noted, hardly any of us from a Western tradition has the slightest inkling what a church filled with icons—which spring the trap of time and bring the communion of saints to life—really means for the way in which the Orthodox perceive the world, and what that alternative perception might mean for our own fuller entering into the mind of Christ. Additionally, cultural differences affect the way in which we understand the world. Westerners know by analyzing, categorizing. Asians and Africans know by synthesizing. Books have been written on these differences, and while there are many subjects on which we have more books than we need, on this one we are woefully undersupplied.

We North American Christians simply do not begin to understand how many ways there are other than our own for appropriating and expressing the gospel. I suspect that underlying our lack of awareness is an all-too-typically American assumption that those other ways are inferior to our ways and hence not worth our time. In the early 1980s, Christians from abroad, under the auspices of the World Council of Churches, visited churches in the U.S.A. Delegations from Ghana and Uruguay reported that during their two-week stay they were not once asked a question about their countries or churches. We should not have waited for demography to force us to pay attention, but the inescapable fact that soon, if not already, the center of gravity of the Christian church will be very far from the North Atlantic, escalates our inattention from the status of the merely sinful to that of outright scandal.

Competition and connection

I have already recounted the story of my feminist conversion. There is a huge, growing, and contentious literature about men's and women's ways of knowing, and distinguishing the politically correct from the genuine insight is not easy. But even if there is a risk of being wrong, there is much excitement in exploring the possibility that there really are profound differences. We have all, men and women, been taught to think of knowing as part of the world of competition. Abstract principles battle for priority. For many women, though, this hasn't ever felt right. According to current opinion, they have known all along that thinking takes place not in the straitjacket of theory but in the detection and creation of networks and connections, in the web of relationships.

In 1983, I learned that the differences go very deep, into humor. I was one of five men in an audience of two hundred at a symposium on feminist theology at Neumann College, near Philadelphia. Repeatedly the room would collapse in laughter, and I didn't see anything funny. Repeatedly I and the other four men scattered around the room would laugh, and nobody else did. Two years later the truth of this humor disconnect was confirmed when I told a group about my experience, and a woman said, "Yes! I was at that symposium. I had started teaching in a college where all my colleagues were male. I went home and said to my husband, 'For the first time in six months I knew when to laugh!'" Whenever I recount this story, the women hearing it don't laugh. They smile slightly and nod knowingly.

No recent event has highlighted more clearly the contrast between traditional and feminist approaches to Christian faith and life than the Re-Imagining Conference, held in Minneapolis in 1993. This was an international gathering, sponsored by three Minnesota ecumenical agencies, to mark the halfway point in a program of the World Council of Churches, called "Ecumenical Decade: Churches in Solidarity with Women." The World Council has been bold in its challenges to racism and sexism in church and society, and as a result has drawn much fire. While the Re-Imagining Conference was not a World Council activity as such, it was closely enough associated with World Council initiatives to be under suspicion in many quarters from the moment it was announced. Planning took more than a year. I am proud to have been the token male on the fifteen-member advisory committee for the conference. I know, first-hand, the commitment to the church that motivated Re-Imagining. The whole point was *re*-imagining *the tradition,* not inventing something new or reviving old heresies.

I believe that historians will look back to Re-Imagining as an occasion when limited Dimensionality broke open. Two thousand women and two hundred men discovered, together, that Christian worship, Christian thought, and Christian community are not a male preserve. Christian imagery, patterns of thought, and rituals can draw deep from the wellspring of women's experience and knowledge. The Re-Imagining Conference was a decisive moment in what I consider to be the history of the early church.

But the way that I see it certainly isn't the way everybody saw it. Many Christians, mostly men but some women, in the aftermath of the conference declared that the people gathered in Minneapolis had in those four days broken with the Christian tradition. In several denominations that had provided money to support the event, the conference became a flash point. The Presbyterian Church nearly split over the question "Should we have had anything to do with Re-Imagining?" Jobs were lost, contributions withheld.

To be sure, there was unfamiliar imagery, some from the female body, in the conference worship, but it didn't matter to the detractors that Genesis 1 says male *and female* are made in the image of God. To be sure, Sophia, the Wisdom of God, was often invoked, but it didn't matter to the detractors, who denounced "goddess worship," that Sophia comes straight out of the Bible.

What strikes me as so strange about the virulent church responses to Re-Imagining is their failure to see that the people gathered in Minneapolis weren't radicals—they were the conservatives, the ones still willing, in spite of the deplorable record of the churches in the treatment of women, in spite of the patriarchalism of the Bible, to stay with the Christian tradition. The Re-Imagining Community, the ongoing network of supporters that is maintained by membership dues and a newsletter and periodic conferences, is not a threat to the church. To treat it as if it were a threat is unconscionable folly.

From women I have learned that even the physical organization of conversation matters. A remarkable reaction to Re-Imagining demonstrates just how threatening to knowing-as-competition knowing-as-cooperation is. Parker T. Williamson, Executive Editor of *The Presbyterian Layman,* wrote to Presbyterian General Assembly Council members in February 1994 to warn them of the sinister implications of round tables in their forthcoming discussion of the Re-Imagining Conference. He said that round tables would promote small group "dialogue" about what had happened in Minneapolis. This arrangement would thwart parliamentary procedure, in which all remarks are directed to the chair from rectangular tables set in rows and are heard by everyone before being rebutted. From round tables, he suspected, only "a carefully edited 'summary' of each table's discussion" would come.

Williamson projects his own controlling methods onto the round tables. Unable to imagine that people might actually acknowledge that they are needful of the minds of others, he can see discussion in a circle as nothing other than a plot by "one key individual at each table." He was right to be alarmed, but not because round tables would beat him at his own game. Round tables change the game, and he didn't want to play.

Round tables blur the lines of authority. When people are seated in circles, it is not perfectly clear who is in charge.

Men were not alone in not wanting to play the new game. Susan Cyre, press representative for *The Presbyterian Layman,* wrote an article, "Main line denial: how our churches are responding," for an April 1994 publication from The American Family Association, *The Re-Imagining Conference: A Report. Information on a pagan conference sponsored by mainline denominations.* In the article Cyre said,

> Unfortunately, the Re-Imagining Conference was not an academic lecture format in which attendees were invited to critically evaluate the speaker's position. Instead, this conference had a worship format in which attendees gave their assent to the content by their participation in the songs, dances, litanies, demonstrations, and rituals.

If I were championing *for a church gathering* an academic lecture format over a worship format with songs, dances, litanies, and rituals, I'd hesitate to throw a stone from my glass house at others for "abandoning the Christian tradition."

Fooling myself

Finally, I am needful of the minds of others because I am so good at fooling myself. T. S. Eliot caught us playing tricks on ourselves when he spoke of people "dreaming of systems so perfect that no one will need to be good." We easily succumb to our desire for neat and tidy solutions, like Avieta Rusanov, the Solzhenitsyn character whom we met earlier, who "always found it distressing when people's thoughts did not separate into clearly true and clearly wrong conclusions, but tangled and grew raveled and divided into unexpected nuances that only lent confusion to ideas." The unexpected nuances are what we do not like.

And we need the minds of others not simply to guard against the obvious, blatant ways in which we fool ourselves. I realize that I have to listen carefully to others if I am going to understand what they are saying. I am not quite so ready to admit that I have to listen to others to find out what I myself really think, who I really am. The senior devil, Screwtape, in C. S. Lewis's *The Screwtape Letters,* has uncanny insights into human self-delusion. To his nephew, the junior devil Wormwood, who is trying to win the allegiance of a man who is loyal to the Enemy (God), Screwtape writes: "You must bring him to a condition in which he can practice self-examination for an hour without discovering any of those facts about himself which are perfectly clear to anyone who has ever lived in the same house with him or worked in the same office." Accurate self-knowledge is a characteristic of mature faith, and Screwtape knows that my self-awareness depends on my acknowledging that "I am because you are," not "I think, therefore I am." I am a mystery to myself, and engagement with the minds of others is one of the graces God has given me for deeper appreciation of what it means for me, and for all of us, to be made in God's image.

So: I am needful of the minds of others because I cannot know enough; what I know is distorted; I know in ways different from the ways of others; and I am expert at fooling myself. I am *ever* needful of the minds of others because I *always* do not know enough, my thinking is *always* partial, differences in thinking have *no time limit,* and I fool myself *all the time.*

An interaction with the mind of another that I remember with special delight took place at the 1974 wedding of a Swarthmore graduate, Harold Trammel, in a church in Philadelphia. Like me, Harold was from Texas, but unlike me, he was a conservative evangelical and black. He had taken my introductory Bible courses, and had resisted, tenaciously as well as intelligently, my presentation of various modern critical methods and the conclusions drawn from those methods. There were times when I wanted to say to him, and others who shared his views, that if they thought I was radical, they should meet some of my friends—within the guild of Bible instructors I was maybe even a little to the right of the middle. But everything is relative, and Harold thought I was way out. Our friendship was firm, but our disagreements went deep.

Though biblical criticism is not usual conversational fare at wedding receptions, in the church fellowship hall Harold told me he had finally realized that if he accepted the theory that chapters 40–55 of the Book of Isaiah were written by a prophet two centuries later than the author of the first thirty-nine chapters, and if, in consequence, he knew the actual historical background of the prophet's words, then he would understand better what God is revealing in those chapters. He thanked me for helping him see this. The theory of Second Isaiah is hardly one of the more drastic conclusions of biblical criticism, but for Harold it had provided a monumental challenge to his understanding of what the Bible is and how we know God. Breakthrough came when he saw that textual and historical criticism do not necessarily disfigure our knowledge of God, and can in fact clarify it. The text may be the word of God, but it is also *about something,* and it is important to know what it is about.

I told Harold that I was glad that he had come round to my point of view, but that thanks were mutual. I had learned much from his devotion to the text, and from his refusal to accept the modern critical method as though it were without bias, without prejudice, purely objective. He had taught me to be wary of the tyranny of the reigning paradigm, the too easy assumption that the latest thing is the best thing. His challenge had made me, in short, a better historian. Each of us had been needful of the mind of the other. Each could say, "I am because you are."

Our conversation over cake and punch in that church fellowship hall would have been gratifying in itself, but for me it was additionally memorable because of what had preceded it. As I was descending the steps from the sanctuary to the fellowship hall, someone tapped me on the shoulder. "You're Patrick Henry, aren't you?" The woman introduced herself, and I recognized her name. Conservative evangelical students had felt marginalized at the college, and this woman had provided a gathering place for them in her off-campus home. Nearly all of these students had taken my courses, which I knew were middle-of-the-road but they didn't. What the woman then said struck me at the time as both funny and mildly patronizing. Part of my spiritual maturing since then has been an increasing capacity to hear care expressed in ways of speaking that are very different from my own. "I just want you to know," she assured me, "that you're the most prayed-for man on this campus."

ON THE CENTER AND JESUS
AND OTHER RELIGIOUS FOLK

Frittered, scattered, without moorings": I frequently hear such terms when people describe their experience, and I have sometimes felt this way myself. I suspect that a sense of being adrift is not a peculiarly late-twentieth-century malady, but in earlier ages it was probably easier to get out of it. There was less space and time to get lost in. The world was at the center of the universe, and the biblical story was at the center of cosmological and human history. A Christian was, in short, at the center of the center. Human nature has always been a puzzle, but our ancestors seldom doubted that there is such a thing as human nature. If you were floundering, getting back on course was a matter of return, not discovery or invention or luck. Coherence is always a challenge, but in earlier times it seemed within reach, because there was a center, a point of reference, a standard, and for Christians that center was Christ, "in whom all things hold together" (Colossians 1:17). Is there still a center, and can it hold?

"No insides"

From many directions there are voices declaring ours to be a time of unprecedented change—or at least rate of change—of unprecedented challenge, and/or unprecedented opportunity. I am suspicious of both optimists and pessimists, mainly because I believe G. M. Young when he says, "The first lesson of history, and it may well be the last, is that you never know what is coming next." Nonetheless, one voice has especially caught my attention, a voice that goes beyond saying that we're not in the center anymore to declare, in the name of Christian theology, that *we have no center.*

The people of the future, according to British theologian Don Cupitt, who counts himself among them, "have no insides." Cupitt considers the notion that there is such a thing as "human nature" to be out of date, a relic of mistaken views that have been corrected by recent philosophers. According to Cupitt, we now know that the world is all on the surface, and the surface itself is nothing but words. What he means is that we are constructing reality at every moment by our speech. I am reminded of Humpty Dumpty's rejoinder to Alice: "When *I* use a word, it means just what I choose it to mean—neither more nor less." But Cupitt goes further, challenging Alice's doubt that our words can be made to "mean so many different things," and her corollary assumption that words can be subjected to some reality test. According to Cupitt, there is no substantial, underlying reality to measure them against. Words are what create our experience, and there is no more than the words. We are hollow—"no insides"—a vacuum draped in language.

The theological implication of Cupitt's argument is clear and drastic: We are as free as God ever was to create what we want. The example of Humpty Dumpty is once again instructive. When Alice says, "The question is whether you *can* make words mean so many different things," Humpty Dumpty retorts, "The question is which is to be master—that's all." From Humpty Dumpty's perspective, the issue at stake is mastery. If words are the stuff of which so-called reality is made, then the one in charge of words—"*I* can manage the whole lot of them!" Humpty Dumpty exclaims—has divine powers. And because there is no standard, no center apart from an individual's preferences, Cupitt, in the spirit of Humpty Dumpty, echoes Genesis with stunning precision when he claims that the new view of reality as under constant construction "vindicates everything right now." This sounds just like God's looking on everything at the end of six days and calling it good.

Oddly, Cupitt says that we have no insides, no human nature, and then makes the entire universe the projection of our desires. He puts us in *the* center, with a vengeance. And there is a further oddity. On the one hand, Cupitt credits us with the creation of everything, while on the other hand he says that we are simply the sum of our external relations. I am entirely defined, he says, by the way in which outside influences impinge on me. Take me out of my context, and I am like Oakland, California, in Gertrude Stein's famous (and unfair) aphorism: "There isn't any there there."

Cupitt believes that we, unlike our ancestors, have grown up and achieved a great liberation. The rhetorical hyperventilation of his book, *Radicals and the Future of the Church,* mirrors his conviction that to have "no insides" is wonderful and to see "identity" as illusion is mature enlightenment. And his view is dangerous. The measure of the danger is in his statement, "everything is permitted," a tacit adoption of Ivan Karamazov's famous declaration that "everything is lawful"— without a trace of Ivan's shudder.

Cupitt scares me not only because his view is dangerous, but also because some of my own judgments seem headed in the same direction as his. If I were to ride "I am because you are" all the way to the end of the road, I could end up at "I am nothing but the sum of my external relations." My suspicion of certainties could, if unchecked, become the conviction that we are simply constructing reality at every moment by our speech. I am something of a radical—it goes with my name— and I certainly hope to have a beneficial influence on the future of the church. But the scenario that Cupitt fashions for radicals in the future of the church has no role that I am prepared to play.

A center without dogmatism

As I have sought to get my bearings in a world where everything moves, two playwrights, Robert Bolt and Václav Havel, have been my most instructive and constructive conversation partners. They have helped me find a way to re-assert the center without recourse to dogmatism or individualism. They are trustworthy because they acknowledge fully, while shuddering at, the realities to which Cupitt points.

Bolt, in the preface to *A Man for All Seasons,* his play about Thomas More, says that we describe "ourselves to ourselves in terms more appropriate to somebody seen through a window. We think of ourselves in the Third Person." Havel says that in the modern world, which has become in both West and East a consumer society, the fundamental problem "is much more than a simple conflict between two identities," one longing for moral integrity, the other coming to terms with living in a lie. "It is something far worse: it is a challenge to the very notion of identity itself." The incisiveness and power of Havel and More—as Bolt creates him—are in their demonstration that identity, or "having insides," lies not in some private spiritual realm sealed off from public, communal life. As public figures, More, Lord Chancellor of England, and Havel, elected President of Czechoslovakia shortly after he was sprung from prison, know well that for everybody, high official and common citizen alike, identity is both gift and task. In Bolt's play, More challenges the Duke of Norfolk to acknowledge some core of identity: "Is there no single sinew in the midst of this that serves no appetite of Norfolk's but is just Norfolk?" and then carries the challenge one decisive step further: "There is! Give *that* some exercise, my lord!" Identity is not a possession to be hoarded but a trust to be exercised, put into play, made to count in the public realm.

We hardly know how to think about the connections between character and public life. Indeed, much of the time
there appears to be no connection at all. The public realm in
our time has been formatted to fit a narrow screen, like a
movie altered for videotape. The vast middle ground, where
society's work gets done with moderate efficiency and adequate integrity, gets squeezed in the public's attention between
scandal from one direction and vacuity from the other. The
motion picture *Wag the Dog* presents a staged war to distract
the nation from White House shenanigans, and the story is
just plausible enough to make us squirm. Garry Trudeau gave
us in "Doonesbury" a George Bush whose presence is empty
space, the ultimate expression of a totally fluid identity so dependent on polls that you can never locate it, because as soon
as one set of poll results is in, another survey is already underway. It is little wonder that cynicism about public life infects us
at every level. The only thing we trust is our conviction that
somebody is fooling us.

Light from the east

But then, as if rousing us from a drugged sleep, a voice reminds us that politics, community, and public life are not
best understood as dirty work that somebody has to do, but as
a gift that God has given us. From a most unexpected quarter,
Eastern Europe, we have been reminded almost overnight in a
fresh and exhilarating way of the great debates about human
and divine purpose that lie behind the founding of our own

country. Is politics a desperate hedge against chaos and barbarity, or is it the best expression of full humanity?

President Václav Havel's 1990 New Year's Day Address to the Czechoslovak people is political talk of a sort that we have not heard in a long time. *Newsweek* even suggested that the closest parallel is Lincoln's Second Inaugural Address. Havel raises the question of "insides," of human nature, when he wonders: How is it that through decades of official corruption, decades in which the distinction between lies and truth vanished as people became "used to saying something different from what [they] thought," decades in which all the powers of the state were devoted to the obliteration of all traditions and the fashioning of an entirely new order, the people of Czechoslovakia maintained a sense of identity? That when the signs and times and seasons were right, they "found the marvelous strength to shake from their shoulders in several weeks and in a decent and peaceful way the totalitarian yoke"?

How can I gauge the difference in feeling about the world between my generation and that of people in their twenties today? When I was in my twenties, Soviet Premier Nikita Khrushchev, who had earlier claimed that the Soviet Union would bury us, pounded his shoe on the podium at the United Nations in a fit of rage. Today's twenty-somethings' perception of the world is formed by the Berlin Wall's sudden tumbling down—almost as rapidly as the walls of Jericho; by the award of the Nobel Peace Prize to President Mikhail Gorbachev; and by Gorbachev's subsequent descent into oblivion as the Soviet Union, between the August coup and Christmas

Day of 1991, disappeared from the face of the earth. Reality rears its head, of course. Tribalisms threaten everywhere. Czechoslovakia is already a memory, split into the Czech Republic and Slovakia.

But the fact remains: There is excitement about the possibilities of public life as an arena for experiment, creativity, and fulfillment. We live in one of those rare moments when, as the chorus says in Seamus Heaney's version of a play by Sophocles, "hope and history rhyme." Eastern Europe has given us a spiritual jolt, has awakened us out of our cynical slumbers. In the depths of political darkness, in 1975, Havel wrote: "Life rebels against all uniformity and leveling; its aim is not sameness, but variety, the restlessness of transcendence, the adventure of novelty and rebellion against the status quo." "The Spirit blows where it wills" (John 3:8) is these days a sober journalistic observation, not simply a pious biblical phrase.

A definite outline

I saw *A Man for All Seasons* in its premiere engagement in London in the fall of 1960, shortly after I arrived at Oxford University to begin my study of theology. I was struck immediately by the way in which Bolt, through More's dialogue, insists on the irreducible personhood of every human being, the essential "I" that we can never fully dissect or pin to a specimen board. In the preface to the play, Bolt says that his intent was to use a person dead more than four hundred years to bring us face to face with ourselves, and the critical acclaim and popular attention the work received, especially when it became a movie, suggest that Bolt accomplished what he set out to do. Almost thirty years before Cupitt's book, Bolt was saying this:

> Socially, we fly from the idea of an individual to the professional describers, the classifiers, the men with the categories and a quick ear for the latest subdivision, who flourish among us like priests. Individually, we do what we can to describe and classify ourselves and so assure ourselves that from the outside at least we do have a definite outline. Both socially and individually it is with us as it is with our cities—an accelerating flight to the periphery, leaving a center which is empty when the hours of business are over.

Fourteen years later Havel made the same point with a different image:

> It's as if we were playing for a number of different teams at once, each with different uniforms, and as though—and this is the main thing—we didn't know which one we ultimately belonged to, which of those teams was really ours.

Empty center; which team am I on? In my years of teaching I read many personal essays by students, which accompanied their applications for graduate school or fellowships. Candor and concreteness were in short supply. Frequently there was no correlation between what was on the page and the person who was sitting in my office. Someone who face-to-face spoke plainly, sometimes even playfully, came across on paper with huff and puff, polysyllabic, passive voice, all bets hedged, and as if from very far away. When given the chance on an application form to talk about themselves, it was like what Bolt said: They thought of themselves in the third person. The students had been rewarded so long for keeping themselves out of their work (beginning in elementary school) that when they were invited to put themselves into it, they had no idea what the question meant. They were startled when I pointed out the disconnect between how I perceived them and how they portrayed themselves. Often they thought they were being bold and sophisticated in their applications, but alienation from their own feeling, even from their own thinking—learned from their elders and masquerading as academic "objectivity"—was actually a comfortable cushion against the risk of vulnerability. As I have already noted, I had no clear awareness of "insides" for the first two decades of my life, so as I was reading those impersonal "personal" essays I occasionally slipped through a time warp and stared into a mirror. I did not like what I saw.

Bolt says that the center was abandoned. Cupitt says that the center was always an illusion. Havel reasserts the center, saying that the most momentous events of our time can be understood only as the emergence into public view of an integrity, a sense of self, that has weathered the most brutal and sustained assaults that modern totalitarianism could mount against it. Bolt says of Thomas More what Havel seems to be saying of the Czech people: "He knew where he began and left off." Knowing and maintaining limits, far from straitjacketing the spirit, is the precondition for freedom. Bolt makes the point clear and sharp:

> What first attracted me [to More] was a person who could not be accused of any incapacity for life, who indeed seized life in great variety and almost greedy quantities, who nevertheless found something in himself without which life was valueless and when that was denied him he was able to grasp his death. . . . He parted with more than most men when he parted with his life, for he accepted and enjoyed his social context.

More was, in the phrase of Robert Whittinton, one of his contemporaries, a "man for all seasons," not because he was a chameleon who could adjust himself to any surroundings but precisely because he had that core sense of self, that knowledge of where he began and left off, that freed him up to respond as situations developed and changed. He could be available to others because he was not in danger of losing himself.

A Man for All Seasons, Havel's New Year's Address, and Havel's earlier writings, which clearly prepare the way for his great oration, offer converging routes back to the center: friendship, hope, and language. We have already met hope, two chapters ago, and we will encounter friendship again, one chapter hence. This is not simple repetition. I deal with these subjects in more than one place because I keep finding hope and friendship around the next corner, over the crest of the next hill. I have discovered that hope and friendship are advance scouts into the territory I want to reclaim for Christian imagination, what Abbott calls the region between "this can never be" and "it must needs be precisely thus, and we know all about it."

Friendship

Thomas More had an extraordinary gift for friendship. As Bolt says with a certain amazement, "A visitor's book at [More's] house in Chelsea would have looked like a sixteenth-century *Who's Who,*" but in the play Bolt portrays not only the More who was sought out by the likes of Erasmus and the painter Holbein but also the More who genuinely befriended all sorts and conditions of persons. This openness to everyone, curiosity about everyone, is what I find most attractive about More, the trait of his I want most to imitate. I was given lessons in it by my father not only in his stern reprimand when I was a haughty college sophomore but also by his example. He could strike up a conversation with anyone, not as a calculating or manipulating trick, but out of genuine interest in that person's world, troubles, and joys. He listened deeply. My father could certainly be depressed, but it was impossible to bore him. I've inherited from my father a high boredom threshold. It's hard for me to comprehend how, in a world so full of variety and surprise, anyone can succumb to the self-indulgence of being bored. Boredom is a virus that crashes the file named "field marks of God's grace."

More was irrepressible. He could banter with his steward as

well as he could match wits with King Henry VIII. And Bolt leaves no doubt that More and King Henry, different as they were—or perhaps because they were so different—were genuine friends. There is a delicious bit of conversation in Bolt's play of a sort that marks true friendship:

> *Henry:* How did you like our music? That air they played, it had a certain—well, tell me what you thought of it.
> *More:* Could it have been Your Grace's own?
> *Henry:* Discovered! Now I'll never know your true opinion. And that's irksome, Thomas, for we artists, though we love praise, yet we love truth better.
> *More:* Then I will tell Your Grace truly what I thought of it.
> *Henry:* Speak then.
> *More:* To me it seemed—delightful.
> *Henry:* Thomas—I chose the right man for Chancellor.
> *More:* I must in fairness add that my taste in music is reputedly deplorable.
> *Henry:* Your taste in music is excellent. It exactly coincides with my own.

With the playwright's ability to make more than one point in few words, Bolt here causes us to laugh at the king's criterion for excellent taste—"it exactly coincides with my own"—and to wince at the sinister implications, for it will be when More's tastes do not exactly coincide with Henry's own, and indeed stand adamantly athwart those tastes, that More's head will be chopped off. Power corrupts friendship. The human warmth of this conversational interchange is suddenly chilled because we know that, for the king, friendship, even such a friendship as this, is subordinate to power.

Havel, in his New Year's Address, acknowledges how the corruptions of power in the political system have eroded friendships. "We learned not to believe in anything, to ignore each other, to care only about ourselves." People were taught to be warily suspicious of one another, and for good reason: Rich rewards, or at least rewards as rich as a strangled and strangling system could produce, were held out in return for people's spying on one another. He continues:

> Concepts such as love, friendship, compassion, humility, or forgiveness lost their depth and dimensions, and for many of us they represented only psychological peculiarities, or they resembled gone-astray greetings from ancient times, a little ridiculous in the era of computers and spaceships.

Our system in the United States has not been without incentives to sacrifice friendship in the name of prestige, or even national security. Thousands of people have uncovered substantial files the government has kept on them, which include many letters from so-called "friends." But the network of suspicion and informing that we have known is slight compared to that of More's England, and almost as nothing compared to the nightmare of communist Czechoslovakia. Still, friendships among us are undermined by all sorts of more subtle power relationships, and by the very lack of a personal center which Bolt describes. If I do not know who I am, if I am nothing but the sum of my external relations, then I am going to be skittish about those relations, since at any point they present the threat that I will become something I don't want to be. I will try to control my external relations, and this means that I will do everything to avoid the fearful uncertainty of giving myself unreservedly to a friendship. Power corrupts friendship, but so does powerlessness, the powerlessness of lack of an identity.

Hope

When I wrote the letter to Alyosha in 1970, I was already aware, though not self-aware, that a leading feature of despair, the absence of hope, is isolation and loneliness, the conviction that I am disconnected from everyone and everything. Friendship brings me full circle, back to hope, which really is the biggest challenge presented, and the biggest promise offered, to ironic Christians.

For a decade, the area where I live has been a case study in hope. Solidarity, mutual support, community, and connectedness have all taken on fresh and palpable meaning in the determination not to let die the hope for the safe return of Jacob Wetterling, a classmate of my daughter's, abducted at gunpoint in 1989 when he was eleven. Nothing like the sustained outpouring of concern and activity in our community has been seen before in the annals of missing persons. The Wetterling family refused to let their pain isolate them, disconnect them, from other people. From the beginning they have said, not, "Why us, God?" but "Jacob is everybody's child." They have welcomed, sought, and nurtured friendships.

"Jacob's Hope," a phrase that still today appears in store

windows and is spelled out every December in Christmas lights, depends on the strong community bonds of central Minnesota, bonds that for many are reinforced with unembarrassed, open expressions of religious conviction. Jacob's Hope has not so much created community as illuminated the community that was already here. Saint Joseph, Minnesota, can tell other places much about how to organize and sustain a search, but it also knows the other side of the equation formulated by John R. Mott, a prominent Christian lay person of the first half of the twentieth century: "Organize as if there is no prayer; pray as if there is no organization." There is hope in this balance, so different from the snide and clipped cynicism of Cardinal Wolsey when he says to Thomas More: "Yes. All right. Good. Pray. Pray by all means. But in addition to prayer there is effort."

Ours is in many ways a cynical time. The publisher of *Minnesota Monthly* magazine sent a reporter to do a story on the anniversary of Jacob's abduction and admits: "When I assigned the story, I believed Patty Wetterling was making a mistake. She should give up, I thought, and resign herself to the fact that Jacob was dead." But the story itself converted the editor, who goes on to say, "I don't feel that way any longer. If I were she, I know now, I would continue on as she has. But I doubt that I could maintain her fortitude." The story convinced him that her hope was deeper, more genuine, than his own sophisticated cynicism: The mystery, he recognizes, is in her *maintaining* fortitude.

Patty Wetterling's hope does not have the hue of rose-colored glasses. She admits that she does not know whether

Jacob is alive, but she will never give up hope that he will re-turn home safe. "Hope does not disappoint us," says Saint Paul (Romans 5:5). He does not say, "Our hopes are not disap-pointed"; he knows perfectly well that they often are, and he has no illusion that the power of positive thinking will put a happy face on grief. But genuine hope, even if it proves to be dashed, does not disappoint us, for it is grounded in our con-viction that we have what we need. As the editor of *Minnesota Monthly* puts it, Patty Wetterling "believes in the human com-munity."

Václav Havel's message is full of hope because he knows the difference between a hopeful people and something to hope for, the fundamental distinction between hope and expecta-tion. The previous rulers of Czechoslovakia had always been holding out to the Czech people the promise of *things* they could hope for—and never got. Havel reminds the people of his country that they already have what they need—indeed, they managed a revolution when they had, effectively, noth-ing, having been robbed of everything, except their identity, by their government. The hope of the Czech people, like that of the Wetterlings, is grounded more deeply than the expecta-tion of a particular outcome.

We tend to think that hope is single-minded, and there is a kind of magnificent obsession in Jacob's Hope. But hope is broad as well as deep, it has arms open wide as well as feet firmly planted. The magazine editor's observation about Patty Wetterling's belief in the human community points to hope's capacity to draw energy and sustenance from a wide range of sources. Hope may be single-minded, but it is also many-splendored. Havel's 1978 play, *Protest,* written a decade after the "Prague Spring" that was so brutally mowed down by Soviet tanks, helps us understand why variety feeds hope. The character Stanek says to his friend Vanek, recently released from prison, "What have they made of us, old pal? Can this really be us?" Then Stanek, who despises the regime but has accommodated himself to it just enough to avoid arrest, says to Vanek, in words prophetic of Havel's own speech to the Czechoslovak nation a dozen years later, "You and your friends have taken on an almost superhuman task: to preserve and to carry the remains, the remnant of moral conscience through the present quagmire! The thread you're spinning may be thin, but—who knows—perhaps the hope of a moral rebirth of the nation hangs on it."

To underscore this talk of moral renaissance, Havel makes Stanek into an avid gardener, and creates an image of a pluralist world radically different from the drab, monochrome uniformity of socialist realism: "I've got thirty-two shades [of gladioli], whereas at a common or garden nursery you'll be lucky to find six." And then, the note of hope: Stanek proposes to send bulbs home with Vanek for his wife, and says, "There's still time to plant them you know." In this one line— "There's still time to plant them you know"—signs and times and seasons all come together in a convergence of nature, politics, and renewal.

Language

Planting, not talking. I have thought long about the Zen advice, "Speak only if you can improve on the silence." But talking and writing are what I do. I believe Don Cupitt is mistaken in his grandiose claims for language—that it is all there is, that the world we inhabit is nothing but a construct of the language we manipulate, which in turn manipulates us. But Cupitt is no fool, and he alerts us to the enormous power language has.

Like all good writers, Bolt and Havel are conjurers with words. As playwrights they deal daily with the mystery that words are simultaneously action and comments on action, revealers and concealers, windows and smokescreens, highways and roadblocks. They would resonate with Kathleen Norris's frank admission about writing "words you are certain that you mean, even when you have to admit that you do not know exactly what they mean." Here is Havel, the wordsmith, on words: "Words are a mysterious, ambiguous, ambivalent, and perfidious phenomenon. They can be rays of light in a realm of darkness. . . . They can equally be lethal arrows. Worst of all, at times they can be one or the other. They can even be both at once!"

But Havel does not stop here. Cupitt says the new view of language as maker of reality "vindicates everything right now." Havel, however, has seen, up very close and very personal, the horrors that a totalitarian regime can fashion in the name of vindicating everything right now. Even though he has full warrant to be cynical, Havel talks about "the rehabilitation of values like trust, openness, responsibility, solidarity, love." And he has backed up that rehabilitation with his life. Havel and the Czech people, and Thomas More, startle me because in them the center has held, and the center has held not by insisting on uniformity, not by dogmatic adherence to a party line, but by the celebration of variety—the thirty-two shades of gladioli in Stanek's garden, More's reveling in the richness and diversity of the life of the Renaissance.

And I am startled the way Einstein was when he discovered that a whole new geometry was necessary to account for the shape of space. It has sometimes seemed "obvious" to me that the antidote to fritteredness and scatteredness would be a narrowing of focus, an exclusion of doubts, mysteries, and uncertainties, for the sake of being sure. There are many vocal Christians these days who think it is my Christian duty to be sure. But More and Havel show me that I need a different geometry to account for the dynamics of human life, where the center expands the way Saint Benedict's vision did when he saw *the whole world* in a single ray of light. Indeed, More and Havel remind me of what I knew on the carousel, that it is in *turning, turning* that we come round right, not in standing still. Once again, the grace of God comes to me as a jolt out of limited Dimensionality.

Because for Havel the center, the all-encompassing center, has held, he is able, in the New Year's Address, to talk about responsibility and repentance without obscuring his language, certainly without claiming to vindicate everything right now. Of the totalitarian system, he says, "None of us is just its vic-

tim: we are all also its co-creators." He employs specifically religious terminology: "We have to accept this legacy as a sin we
committed against ourselves." Such acceptance means that "it
is up to us all, and up to us only, to do something about it."
And "if we realize this, hope will return to our hearts."

Bolt has diagnosed our sickness as the abandonment of
first-person for third-person discourse. Havel challenges his
people to give up the self-serving blame of "Them" and accept the self-enhancing responsibility of "We," thus reversing
the magnetic field in which our language is set. He knows that
the only way from the third person to a genuine regard for
the second person, you—whether neighbor, friend, or even
enemy—is through a recovery of the authenticity and integrity of the first person, both singular and plural. What
More and Havel and the people of Czechoslovakia and the
Wetterling family show me with dazzling clarity is that until I
shift from third-person complacency into first-person responsibility for the sake of second-person community, my language
will remain what Saint Paul (1 Corinthians 13:1) says it is
if I do not have love: the noise of a gong, the clanging of a
cymbal.

Venturing out from the center

When I started writing this book there were two subjects
that I knew I couldn't evade but did not know where
to put them: Jesus, and interreligious dialogue. They are un-
avoidable, because they are on nearly every Christian's mind
these days. Jesus managed, at Easter 1996, a public relations

coup that most celebrity agents could only dream of: an appearance simultaneously on the covers of *Newsweek, Time,* and *U.S. News & World Report.* And interreligious dialogue is no longer an esoteric pastime for scholars; as our society becomes more diverse, such dialogue is the stuff of conversations with neighbors. An ironic Christian's companion that left Jesus and interreligious dialogue out would strike the reader as something less than candid.

And it's not just that I can't avoid the subjects. I don't want to. These issues matter as much to me as they do to any Christian. Moreover, I have taught courses on the New Testament and have participated in a number of interreligious discussions, and have written scholarly books and articles on both subjects. I have even sat next to His Holiness the Dalai Lama while I moderated a Buddhist/Christian dialogue. This setting here, however—companion, not classroom—is different. Here I cannot keep the matters at formal academic arm's length.

But the question kept recurring: Where do Jesus and interreligious dialogue belong? To give each a chapter, or even to put them together in a chapter of their own, would send the wrong signal. The most important thing I have to say about them is that a classic question of Christian self-definition, "What do you think of Christ?" (Matthew 22:42), and a kind of question that Christians are confronting now more insistently than in the past, "What do you think of, e.g., the Buddha?" do not stand alone as uniquely problematical. They have a place in Christian consciousness, but the place is neither privileged nor especially perilous. It finally became clear to me that it is here, with More and Havel, with the grace of integrity, with the recovery of the center, that Jesus and inter-religious dialogue belong. Having dealt with the question, "Where is the center?" the ironic Christian takes Jesus and other religions in stride.

Jesus the mirror

The hopes and fears of all the years are met in thee tonight": These words, addressed to the little town of Bethlehem in the familiar Christmas carol, are a clue to every portrayal of Jesus, from the gospels right up to our own time. Jesus serves as a mirror in which people see reflected their own ideals or, as in an inverted mirror, their own failures. Jesus is by turns friend and judge. Jaroslav Pelikan, in *Jesus Through the Centuries,* demonstrates how various ages have portrayed Jesus as the exemplar of their own portrait of perfection—and how subsequent eras have sometimes thought earlier "perfections" pathological.

It would be strange indeed if we, at the end of the twenti-eth century, had managed to escape from history to fashion a timeless rendition of Jesus. At the end of the nineteenth cen-tury, the one thing most scholars knew *for sure* about Jesus was that he preached a fiery message of the imminent end of the world. A hundred years later scholars are declaring with equal assurance that the one thing we know *for sure* about Jesus is that he did not preach such a message. What strikes me as worth pondering is not the difference in the portraits but the persistence of the confidence.

The Jesus Seminar is a group of about fifty moderately radical to very radical New Testament scholars, who have captured a great deal of press attention. Especially media-worthy is the Seminar's method for "deciding" the relative authenticity of the sayings of Jesus (the scholars vote by depositing a red, pink, gray, or black marble in a box). This form of balloting lends to the Seminar's activities an undeserved air of novelty and brashness. Already in the second century people were noticing that the gospels don't agree with each other, and some Christians created a single, homogenized version of the story, while others, notably Bishop Irenaeus of Lyons, said the variety showed that no single account could do justice to the complexity of God's revelation. Irenaeus understood, I think, what it is like to do history: first to recognize that the present is difficult to explain, and then to acknowledge that the past was equally ambiguous. As one of my most instructive conversation partners, historian Peter Brown, has said, understanding the past "involves containing, in oneself, the confusion and dismay that ensues from the rejection of stereotypes, and from the tentative and hotly-debated elaboration of new ways of understanding human affairs." Brown notes that how to read newspapers and how to listen to conversations while waiting for the bus are skills the historian must bring to the study of the past. The Jesus Seminar would do better history if it replaced its four colors of inert marbles with Stanek's thirty-two shades of blooming gladioli.

The gospels, with their varying portrayals of Jesus—what he said and the settings in which he said it, what he did, whom he befriended, whom he offended, why he died, what happened on Easter morning—already underscore the inescapable mysteries, doubts, and uncertainties at the heart of the Christian story. And it is not simply the incongruities between the accounts offered by the gospel writers that make Keats's Negative Capability a necessary interpretive tool. The disciples are shown time and again not getting the point, sometimes to Jesus' exasperation. It is not simply that different disciples see and understand different things. Particular ones perceive differently at different times. In a passage at the end of the Gospel according to Matthew that gets less attention than it deserves—the introduction to the "Great Commission" delivered by the risen Jesus to the eleven remaining disciples on the mountaintop in Galilee—we are told that "when they saw him they worshiped him; but some doubted" (28:17). We are not subsequently told that their doubts vanished. Matthew does not pass sentence of faithlessness even on those who are *eyewitnesses* and are less than certain about who Jesus is.

Ever since I saw *Z*, a 1969 movie about a political assassination in Greece, I have understood that the inconsistencies between the gospels do not automatically call their accuracy into question but might even confirm their trustworthiness. In any trial, both sides endeavor to construct coherent stories, but a case is damaged if a story is too consistent. In the movie, the suspects use *exactly* the same words in one part of their account of events, and this alerts the prosecutor that he is dealing not with a random hit-and-run traffic case but with a high-level government, military, and police conspiracy to eliminate a troublesome liberal senator. The suspects have clearly colluded and concocted a narrative to which they have all promised to stick. Taking my lead from the prosecuting attorney in *Z*, if the gospels meshed in every particular I would suspect that the story of Jesus was something made up by the church to account for its otherwise unremembered origins.

The prosecutor does eventually extricate from the accumulated evidence a story that hangs together (though a military coup makes most of his well-founded accusations moot). I am not silly enough to propose that all contradictory stories are true or that all consistent stories are false. There is such a thing as historical knowledge, and I'm as interested as the next person in what Jesus was really like and what he really said. But I am suspicious of any method that claims that its filters are the only truly objective ones. I find particularly odd the assumption that the only things we can attribute to Jesus are things that cannot be attributed to anybody else (for example, if a saying of Jesus in the gospels has a parallel in rabbinic literature, it probably gets a black marble). The scholars would say that they are not denying such a sentiment to Jesus, only that if somebody else said something like it, we can't be sure that it didn't creep into the traditions about Jesus from outside.

But this method, brought to such prominence by the Jesus Seminar, and despite their disclaimers, has one really odd, even ironic, consequence. Many of the most prominent voices in the Seminar have made it crystal clear that their mission is to bring to public awareness what they say the theological scholars have known for a long time but have been too cowardly to broadcast: that the theological portrayal of Jesus in the New Testament is, from start to finish, an overlay on the story of a remarkable but not especially exceptional Palestinian character who never claimed to be the Messiah but was transformed into a cult figure after his death. Their method, however, which denies to Jesus anything that has parallels in his time, has the curious effect of making him truly, and implausibly, exceptional. We late-twentieth-century Americans value the unique, the unprecedented, the untrammeled individual; such a person is our ideal, what we hope to see when we look in the mirror. The scholars, feeding our frenzy for celebrity (remember those three magazine cover stories), find a place for Jesus in the history of our culture when they discover a Jesus who can be our contemporary because he had no contemporaries of his own.

History and faith

When, in the eighteenth and nineteenth centuries, historical consciousness began to raise scary questions about the New Testament, some people reacted by imposing on the texts and on their own religious experience a distinction between "the Jesus of history" and "the Christ of faith." The "Jesus of history"/"Christ of faith" distinction is a smudge on reality, one that was tried out in the second century (for example, by those who insisted that Jesus didn't digest so he wouldn't defecate), and is worth no more now than it was then. Edwin Abbott's challenge to "limited Dimensionality" reminds me that Christian faith—faith that God is mixed up in history and messes around with history—is not about something elsewhere but about something right here in our midst that I too often fail to notice. At the very least, I need stereoscopic vision. By looking at both the Jesus of history and the Christ of faith simultaneously, which I have to do since they are the same, I see the depths to which God has come into the world, even to the descent into hell. To use Abbott's terms, I "decline to say on the one hand, 'This can never be,' and on the other hand, 'It must needs be precisely thus, and we know all about it.'" Jesus inhabits the land between "never" and "it must be precisely thus."

This "land between," this room to move around in, is considered by some Christians to be a sandbox for self-indulgent, lukewarm, fuzzy-minded folk who aren't willing, or aren't strong enough, to take a firm stand for "Jesus Christ [who] is the same yesterday and today and for ever" (Hebrews 13:8). But whatever "the same" might mean, it cannot mean that my understanding of who he is and what he means to me doesn't change through the yesterdays, todays, and tomorrows (even, I suspect, the forevers) of my life. The reason that my discussion of Jesus fits into this chapter about the center, the reason that I find More and Havel providing the setting for my thoughts about Christ, is this: My being at ease with not being sure about Jesus, my willingness even on this central matter of Christian faith to live in "uncertainties, mysteries, doubts, without any irritable reaching after fact and reason," is not a grudging admission that it's the best that I can do in the circumstances but a positive, even exuberant testimony to the solidity of my faith.

I say that I'm not sure, not because I can't stop the erosion from outside but because I know, at least most of the time, where I begin and leave off on the inside. I don't have to hang on to Jesus as compensation for a shaky sense of my own self, or, conversely, as projection of a prematurely closed sense of my own self. The center that More and Havel have helped me recover, the center to which the Wetterlings' hope points and in which their hope is grounded, is self-knowledge that can be trusted not because I can't fool myself (I always can) but because it is grounded in a realization that "I am because you are."

Everything, it is true, is in motion, and entire communities can lapse into delusion, even madness. To throw up my hands, however, and say, "Everything's relative, so I can't trust anything," is itself an irresponsible cop-out. I always have to pay attention, I always have to reassess community wisdom and individual insight, I always have to admit that I may be wrong, I always have more to learn, and I must always be skeptical of my certainties, especially when those certainties exclude people "unlike me." A faith that can say the previous sentence is, I believe, stronger than one that claims to know for sure. At the very least, it has as much right to be called Christian.

Christians and other religious folk

The recovery of the center, then, a center that can hold, means that I can take Jesus in stride because I don't require that he fill in the blanks in my own life. What Havel and More have taught me also helps put the relation of Christianity to other religions in perspective. As long as we see "ourselves in terms more appropriate to somebody seen through a window," as Bolt puts it, in "the Third Person," it is easy to ask about the relations between "Christianity" and, say, "Judaism" or "Buddhism." If, however, guided (and goaded) by More and Havel, I have recovered at least a core of personal integrity and identity, the issue can no longer be abstract, in terms of "religions" relating to each other. The issue is not even "interreligious dialogue." It is now Christians relating to Jews or Buddhists, and even more precisely, a particular Christian, for example, me, relating to people I know, for example a particular Jew, Rabbi Leon Klenicki, Director of Interfaith Affairs of the Anti-Defamation League of B'nai B'rith, or a particular Buddhist, Chatsumarn Kabilsingh, Professor of Religion and Philosophy at Thammasat Buddhist University in Bangkok.

There was a time when I was anxious about people like Leon and Chatsumarn, or at least I suspected that I should be. They weren't Christian, and one of my obligations as a Christian was to worry about them. I hedge what I am saying, because my parents did not act, or even speak, in exclusivist Christian terms. But there was enough in the air when I was growing up to make me think if I didn't believe everybody should be Christian, I wasn't a good Christian. I can't date the switch, but there followed on this period of worrying about others a period of anxiety about the worrying itself. I experienced a kind of moral dissonance between what I thought Christian commitment required of me ("They're lost, so go convert them") and a sense that I had no right to such high-handedness. It helped to believe that my responsibility was not to compel others to come into the Christian fold but simply to recount the gospel, in hopes that they might respond. This didn't really solve the problem, though, since I would still be treating my position, my system, my scheme, as inherently superior. If they knew what was good for them, they'd join my team, was implicit in my thinking.

The center of gravity of the whole matter shifted for me one day when a thought flitted across my mind, with a seismic effect like that of my earlier slipped finger on the typewriter. I never met Abraham Joshua Heschel, the great Jewish theologian who died in 1972, but I have read his works and have heard about him from people who did know him. I did, however, meet, on my trip to Thailand, one of the most influential of twentieth-century Buddhist monks and scholars, Buddhadasa (1906–1993). And this was the thought I had: Would I be pleased if I were told, by someone in a position to know, that on their deathbeds Heschel and Buddhadasa asked to be baptized? The conventional Christian answer would be: Yes, of course. But my own reaction to the question was immediate, both visceral and mental, and contrary: No, I wouldn't be pleased. And then, the following thought, clear and sharp: I doubt that God would be pleased either.

Did I in that moment leave the Christian fold? How could a Christian honestly claim that God did not desire the conversion to Christianity of a Jew or a Buddhist? Actually, I went even further, thinking not simply that God didn't actively desire it but that God positively didn't want it. The true irony was that the God who I was sure didn't want such a conversion was the God whom I had come to know in Christ. My conviction welled up from my Christian identity itself; it was not imported. After all, a tradition that has cracked limited Dimensionality with a God who is three and one, a savior who is fully divine and fully human, and bread and wine that are flesh and blood might, especially since we are still in the early church, crack it again and affirm that Christian truth does not depend on Christianity's being the only way.

If, to be a Christian, I have to believe that God would rejoice at the baptism of a Heschel or a Buddhadasa (or a Klenicki or a Kabilsingh), then I cannot be a Christian, because I *can't* believe it. Belief is non-coercible. You can tell me endlessly that I must, ought to, believe something, but if I don't I can't will it against my non-belief, though there's plenty of evidence that the mind is malleable, and there's a chameleon in all of us.

The words of More and of Havel remind me that integrity is more precious than conformity, even conformity to what the tradition tells me is so. There is of course the chance that I'm just being proud, stubborn, pig-headed. The tradition on this issue, however, as on Jesus, is not uniform. Already in the second century a Christian thinker called Justin Martyr, who paid with his blood for his faith, was arguing that Socrates and others who lived before Jesus were, in effect, Christians. According to Justin, the identification of Christ, as in John's Gospel, with the Word or Reason (*Logos*) of God through whom all things came to be, means that anyone who has lived in conformity with that *Logos* is a Christian, whether identified by the name "Christian" or not. And many theologians today are blurring the inside/outside boundary classically drawn as "outside the church there is no salvation." But I want to go a step further, or rather, take another step to the side. I suspect that I would not be doing my Buddhist or Jewish friends a favor by thinking of them as "secret Christians" (with the secret kept even from themselves).

Before publishing his negative assessment of Buddhism in his 1994 worldwide bestseller, *Crossing the Threshold of Hope,* Pope John Paul II would have been well advised to ponder some history. In 1277, three years after Thomas Aquinas died, Bishop Tempier of Paris, seconded by two successive archbishops of Canterbury, condemned more than a dozen of Thomas's propositions because they incorporated into Christian theology elements of the "pagan" philosophy of Aristotle. And yet, shortly after Thomas was canonized in 1323, the condemnation was removed, and by the sixteenth century the church was proclaiming Thomas a Doctor of the Church. Pope Clement VIII in 1603 declared that no error is to be found in Aquinas's work, and the 1918 Code of Canon Law required that all Catholic priests learn philosophy and theology "according to the method, doctrine, and principles of the Angelic Doctor." Pope John Paul II warns against enthusiastic welcome by Christians of *"certain ideas originating in the religious traditions of the Far East*—for example, techniques and methods of meditation and ascetical practice." The pope's alarm is too much in the spirit of Bishop Tempier. It is not self-evident to me that Zen emptiness is more remote from the self-emptying of Christ (Philippians 2:6–7) than Aristotle's Unmoved Mover is from the Creator God of Genesis.

Until very recently it was almost universally held by Christians that God's covenant with the Jews was over (the phrase "Judaeo-Christian tradition," much resented by most Jews I know, tacitly turns Judaism, a living religion with its own story to tell right up to the present, into a prologue to Christianity), but in the aftermath of the Second Vatican Council (1962–65) Catholic thinkers, and some Protestants as well, have increasingly emphasized a two-covenant theology: that God's covenant with the Jews runs parallel to God's covenant with the church, and is neither outdated nor subordinate. Conversion of the Jews is still high on the agenda of many Christians, but for others it is now as outdated as they used to think the Jewish covenant was. Of course, many a Jew who was forcibly baptized in earlier centuries would find this new development most surprising.

Not just "politically correct"

The issue of interreligious dialogue is neither new nor static. This brief account of some moments of transition in "the" Christian view of other religions is certainly not exhaustive, but it serves to illustrate the grounds for my steady conviction that I am entitled to the name Christian while believing that God wanted Heschel to remain a Jew and Buddhadasa a Buddhist.

In stating this opinion, I am not just being politically correct, responding to pressures to go along with multiculturalism and diversity and pluralism. I happen to think that these realities—to use Havel's phrase, "not sameness, but variety, the restlessness of transcendence, the adventure of novelty and rebellion against the status quo"—are among God's gifts to us in our time. Moreover, the question of the relation of Christianity to other religions is one on which there can be genuine difference of opinion between Christians, and it is one that does not have to be decided right now, or maybe even ever. Earlier Christian generations decided definitively that Judaism's role in God's plan was over, and for much of Christian history I would have been considered a heretic for believing what is now a growing Christian conviction about Judaism's continuing significance. It would have been far better if Christians had held off "knowing" what God wanted. One source of that premature deciding was simply ignorance of the human reality of other religious traditions. Every time I get to know an adherent of another tradition, I learn depths and nuances of that tradition that I wouldn't be aware of if I were dependent solely on hearsay, or even on encyclopedia articles about it, just as I hope my Jewish and Buddhist friends find their acquaintance with me nuancing, even complicating, their picture of "Christianity."

In 1989, I helped organize a program that brought scholars of about a dozen religious traditions together for several days of conversation in Minnesota. The theme of the conference was "The Other"; everyone was asked to address this question: "How does my tradition account for the fact that there are many other religious traditions whose adherents are as firmly committed to them as I am to mine?"

In a discussion period, someone raised a standard Christian objection to Buddhism, as least as it might relate to Christianity: "But Buddhism is atheistic, isn't it?" I winced, as did my friend Chatsumarn Kabilsingh. She responded that when

Christians say "atheist," they have in mind a rejection of God grounded in reason or in pride: the sneer of Voltaire, the rage of Nietzsche. Buddhists, she went on, are non-theist rather than atheist. They do not "reject" God or "fight against" God; it's simply that the requirements of compassion and the relief of suffering mean that they believe the question of God to be secondary. The point probably went right past the questioner, who already "knew" what Buddhists thought.

As the discussion moved on to other things, I noticed that Chatsumarn was writing something, and later she gave it to me. It remains one of my most treasured possessions, a reminder that the reality is not Buddhism and Christianity, not even theism and atheism, but Buddhists and Christians. Chatsumarn taught me that God is much bigger than even my most capacious thoughts:

> *Dried leaves are blown*
> *Across the icy lake of Minnesota*
> *The Absolute prevails*
> *For the theists and atheists alike.*

Crossing boundaries and asking questions

Don Cupitt has predicted that before long people will realize that they don't have any insides, that we are making ourselves up as we go along. Were he to write a Companion, it would probably offer instructions on how to function on a blank slate, with no lines, and probably no compass. Life would be an adventure, the way crossing an ice floe in a snowstorm would be an adventure, or, in an image from a humorous poem by my Oxford tutor, the late Eric Mascall, the way "groping blindfold for absent black cats in darkened rooms" would be.

There is another kind of adventure, more sustainable and finally more gratifying. It is the activity of a centered self. Such activity demonstrates the paradox that limits are the precondition of freedom. It is such freedom that grounds confidence to cross boundaries and ask questions you earlier would have been afraid to ask for fear of faithlessness. With such a sense of self I can wonder at the determination of scholars to figure out whether Jesus did or did not claim to be the Messiah, since I suspect that if Jesus was, at least, fully human, then there were mornings when he woke up sure he was the Messiah and other mornings when he couldn't imagine how he would ever have thought so. That's not having "no insides." That's what having insides is like. And the world of other believers, believers in other traditions, is, from the perspective of a centered self, not mainly a field of rivals but Stanek's garden, with "thirty-two shades of gladioli." It's when I don't know who I am that Jesus and interreligious dialogue haunt me, maybe even frighten me. When I do know, Jesus and interreligious dialogue fall into place.

ON <u>THE 500 HATS</u>, BEGINNINGS, MIDDLES, AND ENDS

Dr. Seuss's *The 500 Hats of Bartholomew Cubbins,* published in 1938, the year before I was born, was one of my first companions. I don't remember when I first encountered it, but it instantly became my favorite book and has remained my favorite ever since. For an excuse to go back to it, I have repeatedly encouraged children, both my own and those of friends, to ask me to read it to them. I suspect that if I had learned the lessons of the book sooner, I would have found my way through the world with fewer bruises, or at least the bruises would not have registered as such an affront to my dignity.

The 500 Hats is about grace in the world, though there's not a word about God, Christ, prayer, or the church to be found in its pages. I doubt that Seuss intended Bartholomew Cubbins as a secret agent for Christ, and I don't want to ruin the story for others by planting suspicion of the author's motives. But I find that it's theological all through, and am reminded of the lady who, when Bertrand Russell countered her claim that the universe sits on a turtle's shell with the query, "What does the turtle stand on?" replied: "It's no use, sonny; it's turtles all the way down!" Seussian theology is all the better for being subtle.

"Let him in before the bishop"

Shortly after Theodor Seuss Geisel died in 1991, full of years (eighty-seven) and with eighty million copies of his books in print, a poem by Dick Watts, "God to St. Peter, Upon Learning of the Death of Dr. Seuss," appeared in *The Christian Century.*

> *I wish I'd thought to make a Zizzer-Zazzer-Zuzz;*
> *The best that I could do was a giraffe.*
> *Be sure to let him in before the bishop—*
> *He made me laugh.*

The work of bishops, the work of maintaining, sustaining, and reinforcing, is essential to the life of the Christian community. But the free play of imagination tells us more about God than do rules and precepts. Dr. Seuss, in fashioning the Zizzer-Zazzer-Zuzz and a whole menagerie of whimsical, even outrageous creatures, jolts me out of limited Dimensionality into a world where surprise lurks around every corner. An ironic Christian suspects that a giraffe, as wonderful and strange an animal as it is, is just God's preliminary sketch.

Three years before Seuss died I was with a small group of

friends when one asked us to think of the person whom we were most grateful to for encouraging whatever it is in ourselves that we value most now. Like the others, I sat blankly for a few minutes, but then Agnes Baldwin moved from the wings of my consciousness, where she had been waiting unnoticed for the better part of half a century, to center stage. When I was a child she ran a theater production company for elementary-school kids, and set us the task of making a play out of *The 500 Hats of Bartholomew Cubbins*. I don't remember what role I had. Was I King Derwin? Sir Alaric? Bartholomew? Maybe tucked away in a drawer somewhere is a playbill telling me that I was not, after all, a star, but one of the nameless lords lining the throne room walls. I am grateful to Agnes for igniting imagination in me, or rather, for lighting the pilot. I noted earlier that it was only in my junior year in college that poetry finally broke through my intellectual defenses. Had Agnes Baldwin not prepared the way, I might still be insisting that poets wish they could say it in prose but just can't.

The clue to what Agnes taught me is in the story itself. The action is driven by the unprecedented inability of a young boy, Bartholomew Cubbins, to remove his hat in the presence of the king; the instant he takes it off, another appears on his head. King Derwin, impatient, inquires of his Keeper of the Records, "Sir Alaric, what do you make of all this nonsense?" Sir Alaric, wary, after all these years, of his monarch's rages, answers evasively, "Very *serious* nonsense, Your Majesty." And what else could he say, since "in the beginning, Bartholomew Cubbins didn't have five hundred hats"? The boy had simply set off to market to sell cranberries, and, without ever intending to, winds up disobeying a cardinal rule of the kingdom of Didd. "Very *serious* nonsense," indeed: I can still hear Agnes's voice teaching us how to say it, and her stern face about to dissolve in giggles. She taught me that nonsense is serious, and that the apparently serious is often nonsense.

Right after Agnes came so vividly into my consciousness I asked my mother in Dallas to track her down so that I could tell her how much she had meant to me. What we learned was that she had passed far into the mists of Alzheimer's, from which she died two years later. I was bitterly disappointed that I was too late to communicate with her but can hope that maybe a momentary connection of synapses brought back to her the outlines of the royal palace and the Cubbins family cottage, and even a realization of how she had opened up the world for her students. That I know nonsense, I owe to Agnes Baldwin. She made magic, and let me in on the secret.

I'm glad that *The 500 Hats* was my introduction to Seuss. I have loved his subsequent books, too, but some of them seem to me to be overly intent on making a moral point. They give the impression that the lesson was decided on ahead of time, the story concocted to illustrate it. *The 500 Hats,* Seuss's second book, like his first, *To Think That I Saw It on Mulberry Street,* sounds like a story told for its own sake—one that turned out to have a point. The point is not instruction about what to do, or even how to behave. The point is a set of hints about how to know.

Casting a spell

Few opening sentences I've ever read manage to cast a spell quite as cleverly as "In the beginning, Bartholomew Cubbins didn't have five hundred hats." No one would start off a day saying "I don't have five hundred hats," and anyone who did say it would probably be lamenting the lack. From the first words of the book I know that Bartholomew is in for a big surprise, and I don't know whether it's a surprise to be welcomed or feared.

Bartholomew didn't have five hundred hats, but he had one, and it wasn't just any old hat, even though it was the oldest and plainest hat in the Kingdom of Didd. It "had belonged to his father and his father's father before him." Three sentences in, and we already know that something strange is going to happen *and* that Bartholomew's life is grounded in a tradition. Something like this was true of my own life, too. In the beginning I didn't have the grace of God, at least in any way that I recognized, but I did have it, because others cared about me. Many marks of God's grace were too close for me to see clearly. Bartholomew liked the hat not mainly because of nostalgia, though, but "because of the feather that always pointed straight up in the air." It would be a long time before I knew that grace is found more in delight than in duty.

The first paragraph locates Bartholomew in time: in the beginning, his grandfather's hat, the premonition of a weird future. The next four paragraphs map the space of the story. The space is the same whether viewed from the King's palace on the top of the mountain or from the Cubbinses' cottage down in the fields, but it doesn't look or feel the same from the two vantage points. From the palace, "It was a mighty view and it made King Derwin feel mighty important"; from the cottage, "It was a mighty view, but it made Bartholomew Cubbins feel mighty small." It would not be until my sophomore year in college, when my father called me on my academic elitism, my feeling mighty important, that I would learn how skewed was my own view of the space that we all occupy together.

We know when Bartholomew is, and where he is. One Saturday morning he starts for town, carrying cranberries to sell so that he can bring the money back to his parents. Ordinary time, familiar place. But when he arrives at the gates of the town, everything suddenly changes. The Captain of the King's Own Guards shouts, "Hats off to the King!" The King's chariot rumbles by, screeches to a halt, and backs up. The King fixes his eyes on Bartholomew and demands, "Well . . . ?" And Bartholomew "could think of nothing to say." I find Bartholomew's innate wisdom hard to emulate; even when I can think of nothing to say I frequently say something, after all these years still not acknowledging the truth in my father's aphorism that it's good to know several languages but even better to keep your mouth shut in one.

Bartholomew's silence of course fuels the King's anger. "Do you or do you *not* take off your hat before your King?" Bartholomew breathes a sigh of relief. "I *do* take off my hat before my King." Then follows a hilarious interchange, in which Bartholomew shows the King the hat in his hand, only to be asked by the King, "What's that on your head?" He reaches up and finds a hat. Grasping for an explanation, Bartholomew suggests that somebody behind him must have put it on his head. But how it got there does not matter to the King. Bartholomew snatches it off and finds that it's just the same as the hat in his hand. But the problem persists.

When the King demands to know what all this means, Bartholomew answers, "I don't know, Sire. It never happened to me before." Compressed into this brief interchange is one of the toughest lessons that I have ever learned, and I am still learning it. When I think that I have done something, I may not have, or my answer to a question may not be an answer to what is really being asked. Bartholomew's having his hat in his hand was, for him, sufficient evidence that he had taken off his hat for his King. But the King was asking about the hat on his head, not the one in his hand. When the black students at Swarthmore said, "No more dialogue; we want you to listen," and when my female colleague said, "We want you for an ally, but we don't want you to tell us what to do," they were asking me about the hat on my head, not the one in my hand. And it had "never happened to me before"—or rather, it had happened, many times. I just hadn't gotten it.

Mighty important and mighty small

The King, defender (and prisoner) of rules, orders the arrest of Bartholomew, who is seized by the Captain of the King's Own Guards. In the mayhem, the basket of cranberries that Bartholomew is carrying, the family's only livelihood, flies out of the boy's hands. Seuss deftly reminds us of the different perspective into which Bartholomew is being conveyed: the ride to the palace is "past the bright gardens of the wealthy merchants . . . on past the walls of the noblemen's castles." Bartholomew is going from where he feels mighty small to where King Derwin feels mighty important, and for a while, at least, Bartholomew is going to feel smaller than ever. The King in his carriage has gone ahead, and Bartholomew is told solemnly, "His Majesty waits in the Throne Room."

It's as he wends his way through the corridors to the Throne Room that Bartholomew makes what I consider to be his only error of judgment. "For a moment Bartholomew was terribly frightened. 'Still,' he thought to himself, 'the King can do nothing dreadful to punish me, because I really haven't done anything wrong. It would be cowardly to feel afraid.'" Fear is not, by itself, particularly productive, and Bartholomew is wise to try to put it aside, or at least dampen it. But feelings should not be classified as cowardly. Kings *can* do dreadful things to people who haven't done anything wrong (just ask Job), so fear in Bartholomew's case is simply rational.

I have had to learn, and am still learning, that feelings denied are far more destructive than feelings acknowledged. In the immediate aftermath of my father's suicide, my mother's reaction—"How could you do this to me?"—was anger at him, perhaps also at God. I didn't criticize her openly, but I held her emotions against her. I know now, though, that she was far wiser than I, and she healed sooner than I did. The moment of horror that nearly overwhelmed me a year later can be traced directly to my own reaction to my father's death, my conviction not that it would be cowardly but that it would be unseemly to do anything other than fashion an excellent funeral service and get on with life. I squashed my anger so expertly that I didn't even know that it was there to be squashed. My defense mechanism had been triggered the instant I received the news. So I want to say to Bartholomew, "You're right to feel afraid, and it doesn't make you a coward. The King can kill you. You can move forward confidently, because you haven't done anything wrong, but you have to be wary, because you *have* broken the law. There's still a hat on your head. Don't deny your fear."

The King says that he'll give Bartholomew one more chance, and asks him once more to remove his hat. Bartholomew's reply is polite and honest: "I will—but I'm afraid it won't do any good." And he is right. "He took off his hat—and it didn't do any good." Sir Alaric, Keeper of the Records, makes his "very *serious* nonsense" observation, and the King calls in the maker of hats, Sir Snipps, who sneers at Bartholomew's plain hat and, when he knocks it off only to see another appear, runs shrieking from the Throne Room. Following Sir Alaric's advice, the King calls in his Wise Men. Nadd, who "knows about everything in all [the] kingdom," shakes his head; the Father of Nadd, who "knows about everything in all [the] kingdom and in all the world beyond," locks his fingers across his chest; and the Father of the Father of Nadd, who "knows about everything in all [the] kingdom, in all the world beyond, and in all other worlds that may happen to be," nibbles at the end of his beard.

The stymied Wise Men, something of a joke when they appear in the book, prove in the end to deserve their title. The final word will be that what happened "just happened to happen," and had no parallel in "all [the] kingdom, in all the world beyond, or in all other worlds that may happen to be." I said earlier that science fiction has been an aerobic workout for my imagination. Actually, the workouts started when I was a child and read *The 500 Hats*. Seuss was limbering me up for the occasion, many years later, when I would hear a good friend, the eminent Roman Catholic theologian George H. Tavard, describe, in detail and with deep emotion, his encounter with other worlds that may happen to be.

It was one evening in winter—December or January—in Columbus, Ohio, around 9:30 p.m. I was quietly reading something, and I felt a sudden urge to look outside. I went out the front door. Right in front and above, beyond the house across the street, there was a shape in the air. The shape must have looked like a rectangular box standing upright, with very bright lights or lamps on each side, with orange-like and green-blue lights of a shade I had never seen anywhere. My first reaction was to say to myself, "I am not afraid!" As I looked at the thing I had a very vivid feeling of being observed. After some time (seconds or minutes? I do not know), the thing vanished, though I did not see it go away. One moment it was there, the next moment it was not there. I looked up the newspaper the next few days, and I read that there had been several reports of UFOs on that day in the region of Cincinnati. Whether these were connected with mine I did not attempt to find out.

The question "Do you believe in UFOs?" is for me an un-real, abstract question, slippery from too much handling by "experts." But "Do you believe your friend who says he's seen one?" is a question I can handle. It is much harder for me to disbelieve George Tavard than to believe in UFOs. King Der-win's Wise Men would understand what I mean.

Seuss shows himself a master of comic timing. Immediately following the solemn (though hilarious) posturings of the Wise Men, he slides into slapstick, when Grand Duke Wilfred, a boy about Bartholomew's age, offers to solve the problem. With the instantaneous dislike that so often erupts between kids, Wilfred and Bartholomew exchange taunts about their abilities with bow and arrow. Wilfred takes several shots, yet hats continue to sit on Bartholomew's head after each one. "It's not fair, it's not fair," the Grand Duke cries, and he throws down his bow and stamps on it. It will take me a long time to learn that some problems aren't solvable, and that there's no use blaming others, or technique, or ignorance, or even sin. Things sometimes just don't work, and won't, and throwing down the bow and stamping on it looks faintly ridiculous.

The Yeoman of the Bowmen is summoned. His huge arrow slams through the hat and carries it a full half mile before lodging in the heart of an oak tree. "Yet there on Barthol-omew's head sat another hat." The Yeoman of the Bowmen cries, "It's black magic!" and the King thinks he finally has the right diagnosis. The seven court magicians, with their seven cats, come and chant strange words. When they're done, the King commends them. But the hat is still there.

When the magicians tell the King, "Be calm, O Sire, and

have no fears, our charm will work in ten short years," he orders them out of his sight. The King insists that he can't wait ten years to get rid of the hat, although if you think about it, you wonder why he can't. (You may even wonder why he doesn't just make a new rule, rescinding the penalty for non-removal of hats.) I wrote earlier about my appreciation for both the conviction that God acts fast and the conviction that God acts slow. Tracing my complex understanding of God's speed—the crack of now and the crawl of the ages—to meditations on the plight of King Derwin when I was six or seven years old would be, if not absurd, at least implausible. But if I identified with Bartholomew (and I must have, though my friends would probably have cast me as Grand Duke Wilfred), I might have started wondering why something has to be settled right now instead of letting things take their course.

"It's one of the rules"

In the story's next episode the King's commitment to rules and procedures ironically saves Bartholomew's life. Wilfred says, "If I were King, I'd chop off his head." Later, when Wilfred tries to *act* as if he were King, his uncle will spank him on the seat of his royal silk pants. For now, however, his mean-spirited suggestion strikes King Derwin as sensible policy, though dreadful, so the King orders Bartholomew to the dungeon to be decapitated. Bartholomew, descending the steps and yanking hats off furiously, thinks this is his last chance, and assumes that his only hope is to clear his head of hats.

It turns out, though, that keeping the hat on his head is his ticket to safety, for, as the executioner explains, it's a rule that he can't execute anyone who's wearing a hat. Bartholomew says, "You take it off for me." Sir Alaric, Sir Snipps, and Grand Duke Wilfred had said, respectively, "Heavens!" "Screebees!" and "Pooh!" when confronted with the reappearing hats. The executioner, introduced earlier as one who "seemed to be a very pleasant man," says, in an off-hand way after several hats, "Fiddlesticks," and sends Bartholomew back upstairs to the King.

It will take me years of therapeutic help to learn, in a practical way, what Bartholomew learned in the dungeon: that hope and despair, problem and solution, and plea and help uncannily masquerade as each other. Christian hope is real, but Christ descended into hell, and just as things look different from King Derwin's palace and the Cubbinses' cottage, it is no good telling someone in hell how things look from heaven's point of view. When you're feeling mighty small, what's left of your spirit can wither in the face of someone's well-meaning declaration that you should be feeling mighty important. Bartholomew thought: I've got to get these hats off or I'll die. The executioner told him, As long as you've got a hat on your head, you live; without a hat, your head comes off. Bartholomew did not know what was best for himself.

Nor, ironically, did I on that terrifying night in May 1984, when my name came close to being linked forever with heinous crimes of homicide. Intellectualism, which helped get me into that fix, was also my shield. Like Meg Murry in another classic children's story, Madeleine L'Engle's *A Wrinkle in Time,* "it was to my faults that I turned to save myself now." I never stopped thinking. My mind told my hands to keep gripping the sides of the bed. That hat, intellectualism, had to come off eventually, but I thank God that it was still on then.

Bartholomew angers the King by waking him from his nap, and even more, by showing up at all. When Bartholomew reminds the King that it's against the rules for his head to come off with his hat on, the royal annoyance gives way quickly to royal weariness: "So it can't." The King, thwarted by his own regulations, is on the verge of giving in. But Grand Duke Wilfred is at the ready and offers to push Bartholomew off the highest turret of the palace. King Derwin, though he's surprised at his nephew (the reader wonders why, given Wilfred's earlier behavior), says that it is a good idea, so King, Grand Duke, and Bartholomew start up the turret stairs, in a mirror image of the descent into the dungeon, with Sir Alaric behind still dutifully serving as Keeper of the King's Records and counting hats. At number 451, Alaric notices a slight change: two feathers. Hat 453 has three feathers *and a little red jewel.* Alaric shouts to the King, but the others are too far ahead to hear. It's classic melodrama: Will the message get through in time to save the hero in distress?

It just happened to happen

Apparently not. The three reach the top of the turret. The Grand Duke can hardly wait to push Bartholomew off. But as Bartholomew climbs the last step, King and Grand Duke are amazed. He is wearing "the most beautiful hat that had ever been seen in the Kingdom of Didd"—plumes of ostrich, cockatoo, mockingbird, and paradise, with a ruby larger than any the King had ever owned. Wilfred's rage escalates to frenzy, and Bartholomew thinks his end has come. "Wait!" shouts the King. And then the Grand Duke makes his mistake: He talks back to the King. "I *won't* wait! That new big hat makes me madder than ever." (I find this psychologically more plausible than the reaction of the rest of Santa's reindeer to Rudolf's saving the day and guiding the sleigh with his shiny red nose—"then how the reindeer loved him." I suspect that those other eight were "madder than ever.") The King is quicker than Wilfred, grabs him, reminds him that "Grand Dukes *never* talk back to their King," and spanks him.

Sir Alaric emerges into the light at the top of the stairs, points to the hat on Bartholomew's head, and announces, "That makes exactly 500!" King Derwin asks Bartholomew if he will sell his last hat for five hundred pieces of gold. "Anything you say, Sire. You see, I've never sold one before." ("In the beginning, Bartholomew Cubbins didn't have five hundred hats.") The story ends with Bartholomew and the King each exclaiming to the other, "Look!"—the boy bareheaded at last, the King with the great 500th hat over his crown. Bartholomew goes home with five hundred pieces of gold—will he buy one of the wealthy merchants' houses for his parents?—and the King commands that all 500 hats be kept in a crystal case by the side of his throne.

The wonder of the book for me, besides Seuss's sheer genius as a teller of tales, is focused in the last paragraph. There is nothing of moralizing, no admonition or even suggestion that "if you do as Bartholomew did, you will end up rich." Here is how the story ends: "But neither Bartholomew Cubbins, nor King Derwin himself, nor anyone else in ·the Kingdom of Didd could ever explain how the strange thing had happened. They only could say it just 'happened to happen' and was not very likely to happen again." The ironic Christian would say it was an extraordinary instance of the way the world ordinarily is.

The story can be left there, and maybe it should be. But I don't want to leave it there, because while Seuss's conclusion is blessedly free of moralizing, it is rich with moral implication. The people of the Kingdom of Didd are content, ever after that momentous Saturday, to live in the spirit of Keats's Negative Capability, the ability to be "in uncertainties, mysteries, doubts, without any irritable reaching after fact and reason." They don't deny that the strange thing happened, though I wonder how the Grand Duke, when he is fifty, will explain the hats in the crystal case.

"Not necessarily in that order"

French film director Jean-Luc Godard and Dr. Seuss seem an odd couple, but many decades after I first read *The 500 Hats of Bartholomew Cubbins* I came across a remark of Godard's that interprets Seuss for me, and makes clear that Seuss is portraying a way of knowing. It is Godard's response to someone who told him, "Movies should have a beginning, a middle and an end": "Certainly," he replied, "but not necessarily in that order." I quoted Godard's remark at the beginning of this book, and come back to it here close to the end. *Not necessarily in that order:* Bartholomew periodically fears that all is over, that he has no more chances, but what he thought was the end turns out to be a new beginning.

Godard's remark interprets more than Bartholomew Cubbins. "Not necessarily in that order" is the best shorthand translation of the grace of God in my life that I know. I haven't always thought so. It can be disconcerting or annoying or terrifying to be going along in a story that makes sense and suddenly, or even gradually, to find that everything unravels and tangles. It is tempting to make my trust in God contingent on God's underwriting my own schemes for my story, schemes that would rule out the disappointment and bafflement of thwarted plans, broken promises, death too soon, heartache, communication at stalemate ("That's not what I meant at all"). But if that's the sort of God that I require, I'd best slip through a wormhole to some other universe. The grace of God I usually recognize only after the fact.

Gilda Radner, of *Saturday Night Live* fame, who died at age forty-two after a two-and-a-half-year battle with ovarian cancer, said as much, in anguish mixed with lightheartedness, in her autobiography written during her illness and published shortly before her death. "I wanted to be able to write on the book jacket: 'Her triumph over cancer' or 'She wins the cancer war.' I wanted a perfect ending, so I sat down to write the book with the ending in place before there even *was* an ending. Now I've learned, the hard way, that some poems don't rhyme and some stories don't have a clear beginning, middle and end. Like my life, this book has ambiguity. Like my life, this book is about not knowing, having to change, taking the moment and making the best of it, without knowing what's going to happen next. Delicious ambiguity." These poignant and brave words of a gifted entertainer make clear that Jean-Luc Godard's remark, while it is about the artistry of film, is also about the reality of life. "Not necessarily in that order" is a word of hope.

Joseph, his brothers, and the prodigal son

Seuss and Godard are an odd couple. It is even odder to think of them as instructors in biblical interpretation, but they have helped me to see fresh two stories that have been favorites of mine since childhood Sunday school days. I now realize that Joseph and his brothers, and the parable of the prodigal son, have appealed to me because they are about this grace of God, the grace of this wild card God. Genesis 37–50 and Luke 15 announce, indirectly—so you have to pay attention—that there is a wild card, and it's in the hands of one who can be trusted though not taken for granted.

Joseph's brothers, first thinking to kill him, sell him into slavery. This, they must think, means his story has come to an end, even though they are not technically guilty of murder. They show their father, Jacob, Joseph's tunic dripping goat's blood, and thus trick the old man into believing that his favorite son's story is really over. Jacob refuses to be consoled and believes his own story to be at an end too. The brothers consider themselves clever orchestrators of beginnings, middles, and ends.

Then the brothers try again to manipulate the order of events. In the intervening years, Joseph has risen to supreme power in Egypt. When famine threatens the entire region, everyone looks to Egypt, where Joseph's wise stewardship has stored up food for just such a calamity. The brothers come seeking aid. They don't recognize Joseph, who conceals his identity and toys with them for a while, until he finally reveals himself to them.

They have already lived for fourteen years in Egypt with Joseph's blessing and protection. But when their father dies, they fear that Joseph's anger will flare out at them. They cannot believe the new beginning that Joseph's forgiveness has made possible for them. Now, they are sure, the true order of events will reassert itself. To forestall that order, they fabricate a story about a plea from their father just before he died.

Realizing that their father was dead, Joseph's brothers said, "What if Joseph still bears a grudge against us and pays us back in full for all the wrong that we did to him?" So they approached Joseph, saying, "Your father gave this instruction before he died, 'Say to Joseph: I beg you, forgive the crime of your brothers and the wrong they did in harming you.' Now therefore please forgive the crime of the servants of the God of your father." Joseph wept when they spoke to him. Then his brothers also wept, fell down before him, and said, "We are here as your slaves." But Joseph said to them, "Do not be afraid! Am I in the place of God? Even though you intended to do harm to me, God intended it for good, in order to preserve a numerous people, as he is doing today. So have no fear; I myself will provide for you and your little ones." In this way he reassured them, speaking kindly to them (Genesis 50:15–21).

Joseph's response is, in effect, Jean-Luc Godard's: "Life, my brothers, is not necessarily in the order of beginning, middle, and end. You intended me harm, but God intended it for good." And Joseph himself has had to learn the truth of "not necessarily in that order," for the name, Manasseh, which he gave to one of his two sons (Genesis 41:51), born of his Egyptian wife, means "God has made me forget all my hardship and all my father's house." This forgetting is obliterated when memory explodes with volcanic force, and the beginning for Joseph, as for his brothers, comes after the end, or at least when the middle is well underway.

Just as the author of Genesis illustrates the twists and turns of beginnings, middles, and ends with the story of brothers and their father, so does Jesus in the parable of the prodigal son.

Then Jesus said, "There was a man who had two sons. The younger of them said to his father, 'Father, give me the share of the property that will belong to me.' So he divided his property between them. A few days later the younger son gathered all he had and traveled to a distant country, and there he squandered his property in dissolute living. When he had spent everything, a severe famine took place throughout that country, and he began to be in need. So he went and hired himself out to one of the citizens of that country, who sent him to his fields to feed the pigs. He would gladly have filled himself with the pods that the pigs were eating; and no one gave him anything. But when he came to himself he said, 'How many of my father's hired hands have bread enough and to spare, but here I am dying of hunger! I will get up and go to my father, and I will say to him, "Father, I have sinned against heaven and before you; I am no longer worthy to be called your son; treat me like one of your hired hands."' So he set off and went to his father. But while he was still far off, his father saw him and was filled with compassion; he ran and put his arms around him and kissed him. Then the son said to him, 'Father, I have sinned against heaven and before you; I am no longer worthy to be called your son.' But the father said to his slaves, 'Quickly, bring out a robe—the best one—and put it on him; put a ring on his finger and sandals on his feet. And get the fatted calf and kill it, and let us eat and celebrate; for this son of mine was dead and is alive again; he was lost and is found!' And they began to celebrate." (Luke 15:11–24)

The father in Jesus' parable, with cavalier abandon akin to King Lear's impulsive parceling out of his kingdom to his daughters, immediately agrees to his younger son's request for the share of property that would fall to him on his father's death. The younger son at first believes that his life is at its beginning, but soon fears it is at its end. The middle, succinctly characterized as "dissolute living," is blurred boundaries and hazy memories. He comes to himself, Jesus tells us, and proposes a new beginning. "I will get up and go to my father, and

I will say to him, 'Father, I have sinned against heaven and before you; I am no longer worthy to be called your son; treat me like one of your hired hands.'" The younger son, in other words, has laid out the plot line: My life has already had a beginning, middle, and end, so now I will start all over again, and I am going to get it right this time, no matter what.

Jesus tells the rest of the parable so crisply that we can easily miss its astonishing humor. A scenario with all the ingredients of melodrama turns into high comedy: "So he set off and went to his father. But while he was still far off, his father saw him and was filled with compassion; he ran and put his arms around him and kissed him." His father, by this totally unexpected act, makes the point: Your life with me, son, is in the middle; it never came to an end. But the son, who has carefully rehearsed his line, isn't about to miss his big scene. The stage instruction is "fall to knees, bow head to ground, and say, in abject voice, 'Father, I have sinned. . . .'" Yet here he stands, his father embracing and kissing him, and he goes right ahead with what is now an outrageously inappropriate speech: "Father, I have sinned against heaven and before you; I am no longer worthy to be called your son." He's so sure he needs to make a new beginning that he fails to comprehend the message in his father's greeting: not necessarily in that order, son.

This younger son does not have to start over. He finds, rather, that the middle of his life comes after what he thought was the end. His older brother, in the next section of the parable, objects to their father's feast in honor of the prodigal's return. But when his father says to him, "Son, you are always with me, and all that is mine is yours," the older brother has to learn that his own life, which he thought was in the middle, needs a new beginning, based on love instead of duty.

Václav Havel of the Czech Republic, who, like Nelson Mandela in South Africa, knows that lives which seem to end in prison can begin anew in presidential palaces, warns against the seductive temptation of easy answers, usual orders, what he calls a "mental short circuit." He asks, "Why bother with a ceaseless and in fact hopeless search for truth when truth can be had readily, all at once, in the form of an ideology or a doctrine? Suddenly it is all so simple. So many difficult questions are answered in advance!" He decries "the illusion that the demanding, unending, and unpredictable dialogue with conscience or with God can be replaced by the clarity of a pamphlet, that some human product, like a set of pulleys freeing us from physical effort, can liberate us from the weight of personal responsibility and timeless sorrow."

The film *Schindler's List* powerfully illustrates the resonance between acceptance of "the weight of personal responsibility and timeless sorrow" and the hope that is grounded in the biblically resonant principle of "not necessarily in that order." The conclusion of the movie switches from black and white to color, and shows the remaining Holocaust survivors who were saved by their names' appearance on the list, now almost half a century later, visiting the Jerusalem grave of the Roman Catholic Oskar Schindler. By this act of imagination Steven Spielberg proclaims, without denying or minimizing in the slightest the unimaginable horror that was the Holocaust, that the effort of Nazi ideology to bring the Jewish story to an end failed. The movie and Schindler's life and the history of the twentieth century make the point: Beginnings, middles, and ends are not necessarily in that order.

Probably some people find their lives proceeding along a straight path the way in which they expect, but the odds against all the lines of life's poem rhyming are high. The immense popularity of the drawings of M. C. Escher suggests that we all suspect that on our journey, during our "demanding, unending, and unpredictable dialogue with conscience or with God," we will meet ourselves coming back. We'll go through looking glasses and down the hole to Wonderland; our route will be a Möbius strip, or a three-dimensional chess game.

Forgiveness, repentance, friendship

The ambiguity of "not necessarily in that order" can be scary (Bartholomew Cubbins admitted that he was afraid), but so can the trap of "necessarily in that order" (Bartholomew thought he had to take his hat off to keep his head on, but he was wrong). A sure plan for my life can be by turns security and terror. It can make me as silly as the prodigal son, as manipulative as Joseph's brothers. But ambiguity is not automatically, in Gilda Radner's phrase, "delicious." There are three ways to make it so.

First is forgiveness. Joseph forgives his brothers. He does not pretend they had good motives for an evil deed. "You intended to do harm to me," he says. He goes on to say that God, however, intended their deed for good. Joseph has the right to say this. Had his brothers, though, said to him, "Maybe we meant you harm, but God meant it for good, so we're okay and you're okay and God's okay and everything's okay," they would have been hiding their crime behind a theological sleight-of-hand. But Joseph knew that if hurts and ills are calculated, accumulated, and never canceled by forgiveness, the sum of damage will submerge life. The line from beginning to middle to end will be direct and short.

The president of the University of Oregon, David Frohnmayer, and his wife, Lynn, recently set an example of forgiveness so uncommon these days as to be dazzling. In 1995, their daughter, Kirsten, then twenty-two and a student at Stanford University, had received a bone marrow transplant at the University of Minnesota Hospital to treat a rare and fatal genetic blood disorder, Fanconi anemia. The disease had already killed her older sister. Kirsten suffered a partially paralyzing stroke when doctors removed a catheter that had been mistakenly inserted into an artery. We would have expected the headline to be "Family sues hospital and surgeon for botched procedure." But no, the headline read: "Parents of stroke victim not bitter with University." The story said that the Frohnmayers "want everyone to know that they aren't angry or resentful about the situation. 'We knew what the risks were going in. . . . If this situation were to come up again, we wouldn't hesitate to come back to the University of Minnesota.'" This family was not going to let the middle of its life become the end. And this family is being drafted into Job's league. Kirsten died in June 1997, from respiratory distress associated with the anemia. The

Frohnmayers' third daughter, Amy, though so far symptom-free, also has the disease.

If the first way to make delicious the experience of "not necessarily in that order" is forgiveness, the second is the way of repentance. In 1970, a hugely popular novel, Erich Segal's *Love Story,* injected into our repertory of clichés some of the worst nonsense ever passed off as wisdom, the claim that "love means not ever having to say you're sorry." Love really means not ever having to be *afraid* to say you're sorry. Alexander Solzhenitsyn wrote in 1974, when his eventual return to Russia must have seemed an impossible reversal of the order of beginning, middle, and end, that "the gift of repentance . . . distinguishes [human beings] from the animal world," and that "the habit of repentance is lost to our whole callous and chaotic age." The prodigal son repented (he "came to himself," in the words of Jesus), and when his repentance was met by his father's compassion, what could have been a maudlin scene turned into hilarity and celebration. Repentance may make you look crazy. To throw himself on his offended father's mercy might have seemed reckless to someone who knew the son's story.

The way of forgiveness and the way of repentance can do a great deal to flavor the experience of "not necessarily in that order." These ways are unfamiliar, they require courage, and they take practice. Forgiveness and repentance can spring traps and weave beginnings, middles, and ends into fresh patterns. Their effectiveness can be greatly enhanced if they are mixed with the third way to make ambiguity delicious, the way of friendship. I have already noted that friendship multiplies options. It means that one doesn't have to manage one's whole story oneself. When I think that I am at the end, my friends can keep the middle open for me. When the middle seems to be a wasteland, friends can open new beginnings. The earlier quotation from Gilda Radner's autobiography wasn't quite complete. "Delicious ambiguity" was only the first part of a sentence; the sentence concludes, "as Joanna said." Early in Radner's illness she met Joanna Bull, assistant director of The Wellness Community. The community became Radner's support, and Joanna Bull kept reminding her, "I just want you to know you are not alone." Because of friendship, Gilda Radner knew that ambiguity can be delicious.

Forgiveness, repentance, friendship—they don't guarantee clear order in life, but when mixed together they can punctuate one's story with moments (whether at beginning, middle, or end) like the conclusion of the story of Joseph and his brothers and their father: "He reassured them, speaking kindly to them," and of the story of the prodigal son and his brother and their father: "And they began to celebrate."

ON GRACE AT THE IMPROV

In 1986 I visited my older son, Stephan, then studying theater at Emerson College in Boston. He took me to one of
his classes, where the professor, Richard Toma, an accomplished director, had asked each of the dozen students to prepare a monologue. That's as far as the instruction went. It
could be a soliloquy from *Hamlet,* a newspaper article, a poem
(by the student or somebody else), an advertising jingle, *anything.* As I pondered the assignment, I became dizzy: The
world is a place of infinite variety, and if I could memorize
anything to satisfy the course requirement, how could I ever
decide on *this* rather than *that?* I've always thought that open-
book tests, especially take-home open-book tests, are a form
of cruel and unusual punishment, and this would be the ultimate open-ended take-home open-book test.

It wasn't my problem, though, and the students came prepared. What I saw in the following hour and a half was so as-

tonishing that I can still, many years later, hardly believe it happened ("just happened to happen"). Desks were pushed to the walls. The professor pointed to one of the students, who moved to the center of the room and started speaking her prepared monologue. After a while, when "the time seemed right," another student moved to the "stage" and interwove his prepared monologue with what the other student was saying. And so it went, until all dozen students were in the center of the room, fashioning, inventing, improvising a coherent and compelling drama out of previously unrelated words and gestures and movements. They weren't "prepared" for what happened, but they were ready for it.

Ever since that moment (or was it the hundredth time, the first being in the elementary school theater troupe with Agnes Baldwin?), a moment of true enchantment, I have looked to drama, to the stage, to its mix of the prepared and the spontaneous, the expected and the surprising, as the best source of insight into the nature of the God who created the world out of chaos but didn't squeeze complexity, variety, diversity, doubts, mysteries, and uncertainties out of it, who messes around in history and tells stories with beginnings, middles, and ends, but not necessarily in that order. Just the summer before attending the class at Emerson I had been unwittingly prepared for it when I read John le Carré's novel *The Little Drummer Girl,* which says of some of its characters: "as actors they derived no surprise from miracles."

In that Emerson College classroom I learned how to know God in a way that was not totally new, to be sure, but one in which I hadn't sufficiently trusted. A few years later I was caught off guard again when it became clearer to me what the grace of God really means—or rather, what it is like. I avoid the word "meaning," since it gets me right back into the ana- lyzing, controlling mode. Were I to tell you, in concluding this book, the "meaning" of the grace of God, I would be pre- tending to explain it to you, thus perpetuating the illusion that it—the grace of God—is *over there,* and I'm *over here,* looking at it, measuring it, packaging it. I can't tell you what the grace of God is. The most I can do is to report what trusting it is like.

In August 1995, sixteen persons gathered at the Institute for Ecumenical and Cultural Research to consider, for a week, what it means to be a trustee, charged with responsibility for a corporation or a non-profit institution or a congregation, or any of a myriad other human organizations. We were men and women, ranging in age from late teens to mid-seventies, white and black, one Jew, mostly lay persons. As executive director of the Institute I had overseen at least fifty such meetings on a va- riety of subjects, and this one looked pretty much old hat. There were, ahead of time, the usual twinges of anxiety. There was some disagreement between me and the two co-chairs of the consultation about how to begin, and I could always fret in anticipation over the likely "problem of the third day" (nearly every such gathering has its moment, usually halfway through, when things seem on the verge of explosion or implosion or both). I had long before given up believing that I was in con- trol of these meetings, but I still suspected that I was responsi- ble for them.

The "problem of the third day" occurred (on the fourth

day): People were on edge, at loggerheads; in fact, the whole project appeared to be in jeopardy. But I wasn't anxious, nor had I been anxious at any other time during the consultation. I simply didn't worry about this meeting while it was going on.

The group had talked a lot about the action of God's Spirit in our midst. I've heard such talk for as long as I've lived, and mostly I have believed it, or thought that I did. But in our society, anxiety fits responsibility like a glove. Trusting the Spirit seems, in fact, irresponsible, an evasion of the need to take charge. Jesus' admonition, "Don't be anxious" (Matthew 6:31), is hard doctrine and can undermine its own point if I start getting anxious about being anxious. This time, though, I got beyond the preliminary state of confidence that Bartholomew Cubbins managed on the way to the Throne Room. I didn't deny or repress my fear; there just wasn't any fear, nothing for anxiety to feed on. In trusting the Spirit, as in so much else, "it *is* extraordinary," as Saint Teresa says, "what a difference there is between understanding a thing and knowing it by experience."

The whole context of the meeting was crucial for my breakthrough to a deeper knowledge that I could trust God. The group prayed a lot, both formally and spontaneously. We paid attention to the power of ritual and the coherence it can give to thought and action. No one who was there will ever forget the moment when we each laid a flower on the altar and spoke, as we did so, in appreciation of someone who had served as a trustee of our own life.

Group ownership of the process didn't falter. It was tested

by the logjam on the fourth day. We started to get through it by spending ten minutes in silent reflection. A participant wrote afterwards to thank me for my own role, which I had forgotten, in helping us get to this point. She credited me with saying, "We could take the next ten minutes deciding whether we're going to have ten minutes of silence. We're having it now!" Apparently I could still take charge when I needed to.

Following the silence, one of the leaders offered to turn total responsibility for decision-making over to one member of the group, a woman of quiet demeanor and stainless-steel backbone. She, after hearing everyone's brief statement of hope for what we might accomplish, assembled those hopes and said not, "Do this," but "I believe," and thus got us unstuck. It was the grace of improvisation, just as I had experienced it in that class at Emerson College.

Prayer, silence, trust, imagination—all of these field marks of the grace of God were part of the mix that made the meeting so momentous for me. Most important of all, the conversations were full of humor, which never once in my hearing had a jagged edge for trumping or tripping someone else. Somebody always dominates in a meeting, but it didn't happen in this one. Somebody always feels on the margins of a meeting, but not in this one. We were an ensemble.

As I marveled at the delight, the freedom, of not being anxious, there crossed my mind a phrase in the story of Jacob's dream (Genesis 28) that had been read in one of the group's worship services. Over the years I had heard often the account of the ladder between heaven and earth (and had sung, probably a hundred times, "We are climbing Jacob's ladder," where "every round goes higher, higher"), and Jacob's waking from sleep to exclaim, "Surely the Lord is in this place." But just as Gilda Radner's "delicious ambiguity" is incomplete without "as Joanna said," so "surely the Lord is in this place" is only half the story, for Jacob completes the thought: "—and I did not know it!" I had never before paid any attention to this last phrase. The reality of God in that place where Jacob was, and, by extension, in places to which I've been, where I am now, and places I haven't yet gotten to, precedes my knowing of it. Jacob's dream didn't convey new information. It just jolted him out of limited Dimensionality, so that—blessed irony— when he woke up he knew for the first time (or was it the hundredth?) what had been true all along.

Identification of
conversation partners

On what you will (and won't) find in this book

page

1   I borrow the "as if" and "just like" distinction from Roland Mushat Frye, "Metaphors, Equations, and the Faith," *Theology Today,* 37/1 (April 1980), p. 66.

2   Roger Tory Peterson, *Peterson Field Guides: Eastern Birds,* 4th ed. (Boston: Houghton Mifflin Company, 1980), p. 7.

3   Admissions brochure: Case Western Reserve University, Cleveland, Ohio.

     Godard, quoted by Richard Corliss in Cinema section of *Time,* September 14, 1981, p. 90.

On little brown jobs

5   Yogi Berra's aphorisms can be found on many World Wide Web pages (where this one sometimes begins "When," sometimes "If").

page

6　　E. Allison Peers, ed. and trans., *The Life of Teresa of Jesus (The Autobiography of St. Teresa of Ávila)* (New York: Image Books, 1960), Chapter 13, p. 143.

7　　Christ didn't digest: Valentinus, as reported by Clement of Alexandria, *Stromateis* 2.7.59.3, in James Stevenson, ed., *A New Eusebius: Documents Illustrative of the History of the Church to A.D. 337* (London: SPCK, 1957), No. 68.

9　　Anne Sexton, "Rowing" and "The Rowing Endeth," in *The Awful Rowing Toward God* (Boston: Houghton Mifflin Company, 1975), pp. 1 and 85 (first and last poems in the book).

10　　Annie Dillard, "An Expedition to the Pole," in her *Teaching a Stone to Talk: Expeditions and Encounters* (New York: Harper & Row, Publishers, 1982), p. 40.
　　Yuri Olesha, quoted by David Remnick, "Lenin," *Time,* April 13, 1998, p. 85.
　　Eda Kriseová, trans. by Caleb Crain, *Václav Havel: The Authorized Biography* (New York: St. Martin's Press, 1993), p. 68.

10–11　　Maya Angelou, "The Meaning of Life," *Life,* December 1988, p. 78.

11　　Richard Preston, *The Hot Zone* (New York: Random House, 1994), p. 180.
　　I borrow the terms "candor" and "concreteness" from Frederick Buechner, who puts them together in *The Longing for Home: Recollections and Reflections* (San Francisco: HarperSanFrancisco, 1996), p. 173.

page

12   C. S. Lewis, *Surprised by Joy: The Shape of My Early Life*
        (New York: Harcourt, Brace & World, Inc., 1955), p. 214.
        "No spare ship": Aleksandr Yakovlev, in David K.
        Shipler, "A Reporter at Large: Between Dictatorship
        and Anarchy," *The New Yorker,* June 25, 1990, p. 54.

13   Augustine, trans. by Henry Chadwick, *Confessions*
        8.7.16 (Oxford: Oxford University Press, 1991), p. 144.

16   Diane Ackerman, "A Reporter at Large: Penguins,"
        The New Yorker, June 10, 1989, pp. 44-45.

17–20   "The Meaning of Life," *Life,* December 1988, pp.
        76–93. Panikkar, p. 82; Nelson, p. 86; Brown, p. 83;
        Bukowski, p. 84; Jaynes, pp. 89-90; Mason, p. 83;
        Martinez, p. 80; Ring, p. 90.

20   Kathleen Hughes, RSCJ, *The Monk's Tale: A Biogra-
        phy of Godfrey Diekmann, O.S.B.* (Collegeville, Min-
        nesota: The Liturgical Press, 1991), p. 312.
        W. H. Auden, *For the Time Being: A Christmas Oratorio*
        (1945), in Marvin Halverson, ed., *Religious Drama 1:
        Five Plays* (New York: Meridian Books, Inc., 1957), p.
        67 (in the section called "The Flight into Egypt," III).

22   "The crazy Machine": quoted in Henry Mayer, *A
        Son of Thunder: Patrick Henry and the American Republic*
        (New York: Franklin Watts, 1986), p. 461.

On when it is

26   Stephen Jay Gould, "The Meaning of Life," *Life,* De-
        cember 1988, p. 84.

page

28   General Assembly action, reported in *A.D.* magazine (United Presbyterian edition), 4:7 and 8 (July–August 1975), p. 22.

29   Dante, "Inferno," Canto 13, in *The Portable Dante* (New York: The Viking Press, 1969), pp. 67–73.
The Catholic Encyclopedia (New York: Robert Appleton Company, 1912), vol. 14, p. 326.

34   Department of Energy problem: report in *The Inquirer* (Philadelphia), November 14, 1984, pp. 1A and 9A.

35   Luther and the apple tree: I learned from Professor James M. Kittelson of Luther Seminary that this well-known story cannot be traced back earlier than the eighteenth century, two hundred years after Luther. F. Scott Fitzgerald, *The Crack-Up* (1936), in Arthur Mizener, ed., *The Fitzgerald Reader* (New York: Charles Scribner's Sons, 1963), p. 405.

38   Gerard Manley Hopkins, "The Wreck of the Deutschland," stanza 10, in W. H. Gardner, ed., *Gerard Manley Hopkins: Poems and Prose* (Baltimore: Penguin Books, 1953), p. 15.
Thomas Mann, trans. by H. T. Lowe-Porter, *Joseph and His Brothers* (New York: Alfred A. Knopf, 1963), pp. 3–34.
Stephen Hawking, *A Brief History of Time: From the Big Bang to Black Holes* (New York: Bantam Books, 1988), p. 136.

40   Milan Kundera, trans. by Michael Henry Heim, *The Book of Laughter and Forgetting* (New York: Penguin Books, 1981), pp. 3, 22.

page

43–44   Samuel Sandmel, *The First Christian Century in Judaism and Christianity: Certainties and Uncertainties* (Oxford: Oxford University Press, 1969), pp. vii, 7.

45   Heinz R. Pagels, *Perfect Symmetry: The Search for the Beginning of Time* (New York: Simon & Schuster, 1985).

48   Julian of Norwich, ed. by Grace Warrack, *Revelations of Divine Love (Showings)* (London: Methuen & Co., Ltd., 1901), Thirteenth Revelation, Chapter 27, p. 56. Gregory the Great, *Second Dialogue* 35, in Odo John Zimmerman, OSB, trans., *Saint Gregory the Great: Dialogues,* Fathers of the Church 39 (Washington: Catholic University of America Press, 1959), pp. 105–06.

51–52   Ola Elizabeth Winslow, ed., *Jonathan Edwards: Basic Writings* (New York: New American Library, 1966), pp. 69, 72–73.

On where we are

53   Blaise Pascal, *Pensées,* No. 206.

54   Samuel Beckett, *Endgame: A Play in One Act* (New York: Grove Press, 1958).
Kevin Kling, *The Seven Dwarfs,* a play written in 1986 (see permissions at end of this book).

55   Marcion: Irenaeus, *Against Heresies* 1.25.1, in James Stevenson, ed., *A New Eusebius, Documents Illustrative of the History of the Church to A.D. 337* (London: SPCK, 1957), No. 73.

page

56   Ronald W. Clark, *Einstein: The Life and Times* (New York: Avon Books, 1972), p. 521.

57   Krikalev, report in *St. Cloud (Minn.) Times,* March 25, 1992, p. 4A.

57–58 Alice: curiouser and curiouser, in Lewis Carroll, *Alice's Adventures in Wonderland,* Chapter 2 ("The Pool of Tears"); White Queen, in Lewis Carroll, *Through the Looking-Glass and What Alice Found There,* Chapter 5 ("Wool and Water").

58   Abraham Pais, *Niels Bohr's Times in Physics, Philosophy, and Polity* (Oxford: Oxford University Press, 1991), p. 30; cited in Timothy Ferris, *The Whole Shebang: A State of the Universe(s) Report* (New York: Simon & Schuster, 1997), p. 13 and note 3, p. 313.
      Daniel J. Boorstin, *The Discoverers: A History of Man's Search to Know His World and Himself* (1983; New York: Vintage Books, 1985), Part 4, "The Geography of the Imagination," pp. 81–113.

58–63 Edwin A. Abbott, *Flatland: A Romance of Many Dimensions,* 2d ed. (1884; Oxford: Basil Blackwell, 1950). Quotations are from pp. ix, 3, 101.

59–60 Discussion of dimensions: K. C. Cole, "Escape from 3-D," *Discover,* July 1993, pp. 52–62.

63   Thomas Hobbes, ed. by Richard Tuck, *Leviathan* (1651) (Cambridge: Cambridge University Press, 1991), Part 1, Chapter 13, p. 89.

63–64 Nietzsche, *The Gay Science,* aphorism 343, in Walter

page

Kaufmann, ed. and trans., *The Portable Nietzsche* (New York: The Viking Press, 1954), pp. 447–48.

64   Matthew Arnold, "Dover Beach," in Lionel Trilling, ed., *The Portable Matthew Arnold* (New York: The Viking Press, 1949), p. 166.

65   W. H. Auden, *For the Time Being: A Christmas Oratorio* (1945), in Marvin Halverson, ed., *Religious Drama 1: Five Plays* (New York: Meridian Books, Inc., 1957) p. 17 (in the section called "Advent," III).

65–66   James Bryant Conant, *Science and Common Sense* (New Haven: Yale University Press, 1951), pp. 27–31.

66   Roland Mushat Frye, "Metaphors, Equations, and the Faith," *Theology Today,* 37/1 (April 1980), pp. 61, 63, 65–66.

C. S. Lewis, *Surprised by Joy: The Shape of My Early Life* (New York: Harcourt, Brace & World, Inc., 1955), p. 207.

68–69   Harry Nielsen is cited both from my recollections of conversations and from his remarks recorded, anonymously, in Patrick Henry and Thomas F. Stransky, CSP, *God on Our Minds* (Philadelphia: Fortress Press; Collegeville, Minnesota: The Liturgical Press, 1982), pp. 138–39. I have received Nielsen's permission to identify him here.

70   Erasmus, *The Praise of Folly,* in John P. Dolan, trans., *The Essential Erasmus* (New York: New American Library, 1964), p. 113.

page

71   *The New Yorker,* April 26, 1982, "Books: Briefly Noted," p. 143, on Edward Hoagland, *The Tugman's Passage* (Random House).

72   John Calvin, ed. by John T. McNeill, trans. by Ford Lewis Battles, *Institutes of the Christian Religion,* Library of Christian Classics 20 (Philadelphia: The Westminster Press, 1960), 1.11.14, p. 115.

72–73   Reverse or inverse perspective of icons: Egon Sendler, SJ, trans. by Steven Bigham, *The Icon, Image of the Invisible: Elements of Theology, Aesthetics, and Technique* (Torrance, California: Oakwood Publications, 1988), Chapter 8, "The Icon and the Laws of Perspective," pp. 119–34, and Chapter 9, "The Theories of Inversed Perspective," pp. 135–48; and Karyl M. Knee, *The Dynamic Symmetry Proportional System as Found in Some Byzantine and Russian Icons of the 14th–16th Centuries* (Torrance, California: Oakwood Publications, 1988), Section 3, "Iconographic Reverse Perspective," pp. 26–37.

73   Carl Sagan, *Contact* (1985; New York: Pocket Books, 1986), pp. 351–52.

74   Mary bearing a child: Margaret (Coulling) Miller.

74–75   John of Damascus, *Oratio 3 adversus eos qui sacras imagines adjiciunt* 34, Patrologia Graeca 94.1353AB.

75   Theodore of Studios, *Antirrheticus 1,* Patrologia Graeca 99.344 BC.

76   Athanasius, *On the Incarnation of The Word of God,* Chapter 54.

page

Leonid Ouspensky, *Theology of the Icon* (Crestwood, New York: St. Vladimir's Seminary Press, 1978), pp. 210–11.

On paying attention

81–82   Ciardi's words (which I have generalized), from a letter that he wrote to Vince Clemente, served as the basis for Clemente's "'A Man Is What He Does with His Attention': An Interview with John Ciardi," *Poesis: A Journal of Criticism,* 7/2 (1986), reprinted in Clemente, ed., *John Ciardi: Measure of the Man* (Fayetteville: The University of Arkansas Press, 1987), pp. 213–28.

82–83   Mark Vonnegut, *The Eden Express* (New York: Praeger Publishers, 1975), pp. ix, 92.

83   John Ashbery, "The Skaters," from the collection *Rivers and Mountains* (1967), included in Ashbery, *The Mooring of Starting Out: The First Five Books of Poetry* (Hopewell, New Jersey: The Ecco Press, 1997), p. 199.

84–86   Louis Ginzberg, *Legends of the Bible* (Philadelphia: Jewish Publication Society of America, 1978), p. 311.

86–88   Danilo Kiš, "The Encyclopedia of the Dead (A Whole Life)," in Kiš, trans. by Michael Henry Heim, *The Encyclopedia of the Dead* (New York: Penguin Books, 1991), pp. 39–65. Quotations are from pp. 41–42, 44, 51.

88–89   Milan Kundera, trans. by Michael Henry Heim, *The Book of Laughter and Forgetting* (New York: Penguin Books, 1981), pp. 7, 17.

page

95–96   Scholastica: Gregory the Great, *Second Dialogue* 33, in
Odo John Zimmerman, OSB, trans., *Saint Gregory
the Great: Dialogues,* Fathers of the Church 39 (Washington: Catholic University of America Press, 1959),
pp. 102–03.

99   Robert L. Scott, Jr., *God Is My Co-Pilot* (New York:
Scribner, 1943).

101   Time "a hangman's rack": Jane Halsema.

<h2 style="text-align:center">On hoping and praying</h2>

108   John le Carré, *Our Game* (New York: Alfred A.
Knopf, 1995) p. 250.

109   Negative Capability: Letter No. 45, in Hyder Edward
Rollins, ed., *The Letters of John Keats 1814–1821* (Cambridge: Harvard University Press, 1958), Volume 1, p.
193.

109–117 Fyodor Dostoevsky, trans. by Constance Garnett, *The
Brothers Karamazov* (New York: Vintage Books, 1955),
pp. 278, 289–90, 386, 407. Aleksandr I. Solzhenitsyn,
trans. by Rebecca Frank, *The Cancer Ward* (New
York: Dell Publishing Co., Inc., 1967), pp. 15, 103,
277, 314, 336, 401, 441, 485, 496, 520, 538.

117   Senator Scott, *Philadelphia Evening Bulletin,* December 31, 1972.

121   Lawrence M. Krauss, *The Physics of Star Trek* (New
York: Basic Books, 1995), p. 23.

page

122   Kurt Vonnegut, Jr., *Slaughterhouse-Five, or The Children's Crusade: A Duty-Dance with Death* (1968; New York: Dell Publishing Co., 1971), pp. 73–75.

123–124 Robert Coles, *The Spiritual Life of Children* (Boston: Houghton Mifflin Company, 1990).

128   Rex Warner, trans., *The Prometheus Bound of Aeschylus* (London: The Bodley Head, 1947), p. 43 (line 778).

132   Cartoon: drawn by Mick Stevens, *The New Yorker,* October 9, 1995, p. 90.

On why I am (because you are)

135   Descartes, *cogito ergo sum, Discourse on Method,* Part 4.

136   "Figure out my mind": Jane Halsema.
         Jean-Paul Sartre, trans. by Stuart Gilbert, *No Exit* (1944), in *No Exit and Three Other Plays* (New York: Vintage International, 1989), p. 45.

137   "It suddenly occurred to me": Alice (Macneal) Carli.

139–143 Timothy Fry, OSB, ed., *RB 1980: The Rule of St. Benedict in Latin and English with Notes* (Collegeville, Minnesota: The Liturgical Press, 1981), Prologue, p. 165; Chapter 2, p. 177; Chapter 3, pp. 179–81; Chapters 9–18, pp. 203–15; Chapter 48, pp. 249–53; Chapter 72, pp. 293–95.

144   Athanasius, trans. by Robert T. Meyer, *The Life of Saint Anthony,* Ancient Christian Writers 10 (New York: Newman Press, 1978).

page

148–149 Joan Chittister, OSB, Stephanie Campbell, OSB, Mary Collins, OSB, Ernestine Johann, OSB, and Johnette Putnam, OSB, *Climb Along the Cutting Edge: An Analysis of Change in Religious Life* (New York: Paulist Press, 1977).

149   Robert N. Bellah, Richard Madsen, William M. Sullivan, Ann Swidler, and Steven M. Tipton, *Habits of the Heart: Individualism and Commitment in American Life* (1985; New York: Harper & Row, Publishers, Perennial Library, 1986), section on "Communities of Memory," pp. 152–55.

Garrison Keillor, "The Meaning of Life," *Life,* December 1988, pp. 82–83.

151   Second-century taunt: Celsus, in Henry Chadwick, ed. and trans., *Origen Contra Celsum* (Cambridge: Cambridge University Press, 1965), p. 158.

152   Jaroslav Pelikan, *The Emergence of the Catholic Tradition (100–600),* Volume 1 of *The Christian Tradition: A History of the Development of Doctrine* (Chicago: The University of Chicago Press, 1971), p. 9.

153   "Ever needful prayer": Drusilla M. Gillespie.

155–56 Robert Buckhout, "Eyewitness Testimony," *Scientific American* 231/6 (December 1974), pp. 23–31.

156   Dorotheos of Gaza, trans. by Eric P. Wheeler, *Discourses and Sayings,* Cistercian Studies Series 33 (Kalamazoo, Michigan: Cistercian Publications, 1977), p. 246.

Seeing and expecting: Stefi Weisburd, "A Fault of Youth," *Science News,* 127/23 (June 8, 1985), p. 363.

page

158–59   American uninterest in others: Fred Wilson, quoted in Reinhild Traitler, "Preparing for Vancouver," *The Ecumenical Review,* 35/2 (April 1983), p. 126.

162–63   I have consulted Williamson's letter to General Assembly Council Members, dated Friday, February 4, 1994, in a copy in the archives of the Re-Imagining Community, Minneapolis.

163   The quotation from Susan Cyre's article is on pp. 14–15 of the Report.
T. S. Eliot, "Choruses from *The Rock*" 6, in *The Complete Poems and Plays 1909–1950* (New York: Harcourt, Brace and Company, 1952), p. 106.

164   C. S. Lewis, *The Screwtape Letters* (New York: Macmillan Publishing Co., Inc., 1974), III, p. 16.

On the center and Jesus and other religious folk

170   ". . . you never know": quoted in W. D. Handcock, introduction to *G. M. Young, Victorian Essays* (London: Oxford University Press, 1962), p. 10.

170–72   Don Cupitt, *Radicals and the Future of the Church* (London: SCM Press, Ltd., 1989), pp. 19, 98, 141, 157.

171   Lewis Carroll, *Through the Looking Glass,* Chapter 6 ("Humpty Dumpty").

172   Fyodor Dostoevsky, trans. by Constance Garnett, *The Brothers Karamazov* (New York: Vintage Books, 1955), p. 312.

173–82   Robert Bolt, *A Man for All Seasons: A Play in Two Acts*

page

(New York: Random House, 1962), pp. v, xi–xiii, xv, 55–56, 123–24.

172–89   Václav Havel, *Open Letters: Selected Writings 1965–1990* (New York: Alfred A. Knopf, 1991): "The Power of the Powerless" (1978), pp. 145, 210; "New Year's Address" (1990), pp. 391–92; "Dear Dr. Husák" (1975), p. 71; "'It Always Makes Sense to Tell the Truth': An Interview with Jiří Lederer" (1975), p. 95; "A Word About Words" (1989), p. 381. *Protest* (first published in Czech, 1978; Eng. trans. by Vera Blackwell, 1984), in *The Garden Party and Other Plays* (New York: Grove Press, 1993), pp. 245–49.

175   *Newsweek,* January 15, 1990, p. 42.

176   Seamus Heaney, *The Cure at Troy: A Version of Sophocles's Philoctetes* (London: Faber and Faber in association with Field Day, 1990), p. 77 (in a speech of the Chorus).

184   Prayer and organization: John R. Mott, cited in Robert S. Bilheimer, *Breakthrough: The Emergence of the Ecumenical Tradition* (Grand Rapids: William B. Eerdmans Publishing Company; Geneva: WCC Publications, 1989), p. 4.

Leonard Witt, "Editor's Note," *Minnesota Monthly,* October 1990, p. 8.

187   Kathleen Norris, *Amazing Grace: A Vocabulary of Faith* (New York: Riverhead Books, 1998), p. 377.

192   Irenaeus, *Against Heresies* 3.11.7–9, in Cyril C. Richardson, ed., *Early Christian Fathers,* Library of

page

Christian Classics 1 (Philadelphia: The Westminster Press, 1953), pp. 381–84.

Peter Brown, *Religion and Society in the Age of Saint Augustine* (London: Faber and Faber, 1972), p. 20.

200   Justin Martyr, *First Apology* 46, in Richardson, *Early Christian Fathers,* pp. 271–72.

201   Pope John Paul II, *Crossing the Threshold of Hope* (New York: Alfred A. Knopf, 1994), chapter entitled "Buddha?", pp. 84–90, at pp. 89–90 (italics Popev's).

205   E. L. Mascall, *Pi in the High* (London: The Faith Press, 1959), "Little Gleaning," p. 7.

On <u>The 500 Hats</u>, beginnings, middles, and ends

207–222 Dr. Seuss, *The 500 Hats of Bartholomew Cubbins* (1938; New York: The Vanguard Press, 1965), no page numbering.

208   The turtle story is recounted by Timothy Ferris, *The Whole Shebang: A State of the Universe(s) Report* (New York: Simon & Schuster, 1997), p. 263, who calls it apocryphal.

208–09 Dick Watts, *The Christian Century,* 108/32 (November 6, 1991), p. 1030.

216   I heard Fr. Tavard say words very like these during a consultation at the Institute for Ecumenical and Cultural Research. I asked whether I could identify him here as the source of the account. He replied: "I have

page

never written about my experience, but I have not made it a secret." He gave me permission to use his name, and sent a brief written recollection which I have included in the text.

219   Madeleine L'Engle, *A Wrinkle in Time* (New York: Farrar, Straus and Giroux, 1962), p. 153.

222   Godard, cited by Richard Corliss in Cinema section of *Time,* September 14, 1981, p. 90.

223–24   Gilda Radner, *It's Always Something* (1989; New York: Avon Books, 1990), p. 268.

229   Václav Havel, "Anatomy of a Reticence" (April 1985), in *Open Letters: Selected Writings 1965–1990* (New York: Alfred A. Knopf, 1991), pp. 301–02.

231–32   Frohnmayers: article by Gordon Slovut, *Star Tribune* (Minneapolis), April 28, 1995, pp. 1B, 4B. Kirsten's death: AP dispatch, *St. Cloud (Minn.) Times,* June 21, 1997, p. 8A.

232   Erich Segal, *Love Story* (New York: Harper & Row, 1970), pp. 91, 131.
Alexander Solzhenitsyn, "Repentance and Self-Limitation in the Life of Nations," in Solzhenitsyn, ed., *From Under the Rubble* (Boston: Little Brown, 1976), p. 106.

233   Radner, *It's Always Something,* pp. 80–81, 137.

On grace at The Improv

236   John le Carré, *The Little Drummer Girl* (New York: Alfred A. Knopf, 1983), p. 48.

Index of field marks
of the grace of God

Included in this index are the chapter subheadings, printed in boldface type.

Thanks for help

I am grateful to those who read all or part of the text at various stages of its gestation and maturing and made suggestions from the molecular to the anatomical: Sarah Bancroft, Magdaline Bovis, Joan Chittister, OSB, Mary Jane Crook, Gisela D'Andrea, Tom Duncanson, Vera Duncanson, Rachel Durkee, David Dwyer, Gay Grissom, Grant Grissom, Jon Hassler, Clark Hendley, Ellen Josephs, Peggy Lindsey, Robyn Lingen, Colin McGinnis, Jay Meek, Martha Meek, Terry Muck, Kathleen Norris, Dolores Schuh, CHM, Susan Snyder, Wilfred Theisen, OSB, Krista Weedman Tippett, Linwood Urban, Nancy Urban, and Lydia Veliko.

My wife, Pat Welter, has been reader, encourager, and advocate of clarity. The book is for her.

Leighton Whitaker of Wallingford, Pennsylvania, and Toni Murphy of Saint Cloud, Minnesota, my therapists, aren't responsible for this book, but they are responsible in a big way for my becoming the person who could write it.

Cindy Spiegel is the editor every writer dreams of. Literary theory talks about the "ideal reader." I doubted that such a creature existed until I got my manuscript back from Cindy. On nearly every page she has helped me say better what it was that I wanted to say. A few days after I received the first package from her she called to ask my reaction to her markings. I said that I expected to contest about two percent of her suggestions. Her response belongs in an anthology of editorial aphorisms: "Two percent is about right." Cindy, like every editor, has help. Her assistant, Erin Bush, is unfailingly gracious and manages always to keep urgency on the near side of panic.

Parts of the book, at early stages, were tried out in public forums. Particularly helpful to me were the audiences of the Great Plains Institute of Theology in Richardton, North Dakota, and the Newman Center at the University of Minnesota—Morris.

The Board of Directors of the Institute for Ecumenical and Cultural Research graciously and generously considers writing to be part of my job, and I am very grateful for their encouragement.

Patrick Henry is also the author of *New Directions in New Testament Study* (Westminster Press, 1979, SCM Press, 1980), the co-author (with Thomas F. Stransky, CSP) of *God on Our Minds* (Fortress Press and The Liturgical Press, 1982), the editor of *Schools of Thought in the Christian Tradition* (Fortress Press, 1984), and the co-author (with Donald K. Swearer) of *For the Sake of the World: The Spirit of Buddhist and Christian Monasticism* (Fortress Press and The Liturgical Press, 1989). He was a professor of religion at Swarthmore College for seventeen years. He is now the executive director of the Institute for Ecumenical and Cultural Research at Saint John's Abbey and University in Collegeville, Minnesota. His wife, Pat Welter, is principal of North Junior High School in Saint Cloud, Minnesota. He has two sons and two daughters and a stepdaughter: Stephan Marshall Henry, Miranda Gail Henry, Christina Rose Welter, Juliet May Henry, and Brendan Wilfred Henry.

Some portions of this book are excerpted and edited from articles I have previously published. Grateful acknowledgment is made for permission to use the material here.

"Ever Needful of the Minds of Others," *Occasional Papers* 27 (May 1987), and "When Is It? Reflections on a Trip Around the World," *Oc-*

casional Papers 34 (May 1990), by permission of the Institute for Ecumenical and Cultural Research.

"The Ground Swell's Bell Over the Ebbing Sea's Roar: The Sound of Monasticism in Our Time," in Renée Branigan, OSB, ed., *The Proceedings of the American Benedictine Academy Convention, August 8–11, 1990, Yankton, South Dakota,* Volume 1, New Series (Mott, North Dakota: Eido Printing, 1991), pp. 11–20, by permission of the American Benedictine Academy.

"Homosexuals: Identity and Dignity," 33/1 (April 1976), pp. 33–39; "Holy Saturday 4/2/88," 45/4 (January 1989), p. 429; and "The Carousel," 49/2 (July 1992), pp. 246–48, by permission of *Theology Today.*

"The Last Word: A Good Friday Meditation on Luke 24:36." Copyright 1981 Christian Century Foundation. Reprinted by permission from the April 8, 1981, issue of *The Christian Century,* pp. 385–87.

"Psychological Services Challenges the Academy," 1/1 (Fall 1986), pp. 43–51, by permission of *Journal of College Student Psychotherapy.*

"Religion and the Academic Profession—The Strange Loop," *Religion and Intellectual Life,* 2/2 (Winter 1985), pp. 105–20; "On Paying Attention," *Religion and Intellectual Life,* 4/2 (Winter 1987), pp. 39–47; and "Not Necessarily in That Order," *Cross Currents,* 46/1 (Spring 1996), pp. 88–96, by permission of the Association for Religion and Intellectual Life.

"Why *Life* Says We Are Here." Copyright 1989 Christian Century Foundation. Reprinted by permission from the May 24–31, 1989, issue of *The Christian Century,* pp. 562–63.

"Can the Center Hold? Thomas More and Václav Havel on Social and Personal Integrity," in William Caferro and Duncan G. Fisher, eds., *The Unbounded Community: Papers in Christian Ecumenism in Honor of Jaroslav Pelikan* (70th birthday Festschrift) (New York and London: Garland Publishing, Inc., 1996), pp. 149–62, by permission of Garland Publishing, Inc.